Don't let the overload of information in all-in-one Guides hold you back. This meticulously crafted book zeroes in exclusively on Microsoft Word and Excel, offering a deep dive into their features to ensure you gain meaningful insights and practical knowledge.

Whether you're a learner, an avid reader, a beginner, or an experienced user, this guide is tailored for you. Let it boost your confidence, ignite your creativity, and lead you effortlessly toward mastering Microsoft Word and Excel.

# Table of Contents

# Introduction to Microsoft Office 365

E mbarking on your journey with Microsoft Office 365 begins with selecting the right plan, installing the software on your devices, and personalizing your account to suit your needs. This guide will walk you through the entire process, providing detailed, instructor-style guidance to ensure a seamless setup.

## Getting Started with Microsoft Office 365

### Choosing the Right Office 365 Subscription Plan

Microsoft Office 365 offers subscription options tailored to various users. Here's how to choose the best fit:

1. Personal Plan:
Designed for individual users, this plan includes the full suite of Office applications (Word, Excel, PowerPoint, etc.) and 1TB of OneDrive storage. Ideal for personal projects and light work-related tasks.

2. Family Plan:

Perfect for households, this option supports up to six users. Each person receives their own 1TB of OneDrive storage, making it a cost-effective choice for families.

3. Business Plan:

Created for small businesses, this plan provides access to Office apps, business email via Outlook, 1TB of OneDrive storage per user, and advanced collaboration tools and security features.

4. Education Plan:

Students and teachers may qualify for free access to Office 365 Education. This plan includes Word, Excel, PowerPoint, OneNote, Teams, and OneDrive.

Visit Microsoft's subscription page at https://www.microsoft.com/en-us/microsoft-365/get-started-with-office-365 to compare plans and select the one that best suits your requirements.

## Installing Office 365 on Various Devices

Once you've chosen a plan, follow these instructions to install Office 365 on your device:

## For Windows Users:

1. Navigate to the Microsoft Office download page and sign in with your Microsoft account. If you don't have one, create an account.
2. Click the Install Office button to download the installation file.
3. Open the file and follow the on-screen prompts to complete the installation.
4. Launch any Office app, such as Word, and sign in to activate your subscription.

## For Mac Users:

1. Visit the Office download page for Mac and sign in.
2. Download the installer specific to macOS.
3. Run the installer and follow the prompts to set up Office.

4. Open an Office app and sign in to complete the activation process.

**For Mobile Devices (iOS and Android):**

1. Open the App Store (iOS) or Google Play Store (Android).
2. Search for and download Office apps like Word, Excel, or PowerPoint.
3. Sign in with your Microsoft account to access all features.

## Navigating the Office 365 Dashboard

After logging in, you'll land on the Office 365 homepage. Here's what you need to know:

**Homepage Overview:**

- Access frequently used apps such as Word, Excel, and PowerPoint via large icons.
- Customize your homepage by pinning your favorite apps for quick access.
- Use the search bar at the top to find documents, apps, or collaborators.

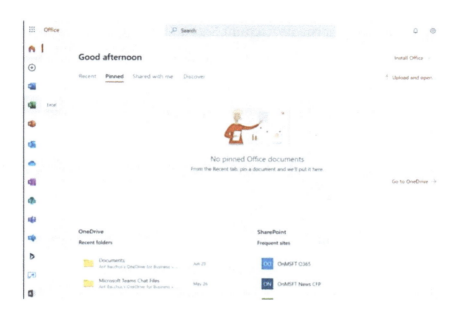

App Launcher:

Located in the top-left corner, this "waffle" icon opens the full menu of available apps, including Teams, OneDrive, Publisher, and Access.

Settings Menu:

Click your profile icon in the top-right corner to access account settings. From here, you can manage notifications, themes, and language preferences.

## Creating and Managing Your Microsoft Account

A Microsoft account is essential for using Office 365. Follow these steps to create one:

1. Visit the Microsoft Account Signup page.
2. Enter your email address or create a new Outlook or Hotmail account.
3. Choose a strong password and complete the verification process.
4. Once your account is created, log in to Office 365 with your new credentials.

Manage your account settings, update personal information, and enhance security by visiting the Microsoft Account Management page.

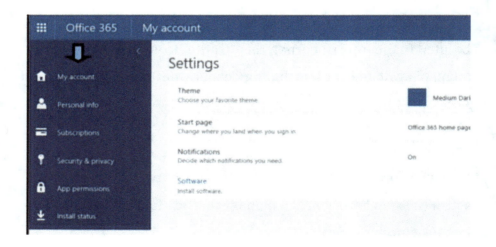

## Personalizing Your Office 365 Profile

Enhance your user experience by personalizing your profile:

- Profile Picture: Click your profile icon, select Edit Profile, and upload a photo.
- Language Settings: Navigate to Settings > Language and Region to select your preferred language.
- Security: Enable two-factor authentication (2FA) to protect your account from unauthorized access.

# Part 1: Microsoft Word for Beginners

# Chapter 1. Getting Started with Microsoft Word

Microsoft Word is a word-processing application that helps you create, format, and edit documents. Whether you're drafting a letter, creating a resume, or compiling a report, Word simplifies the process. It's an essential tool for students, professionals, and anyone who needs to produce polished written content.

Some of the key features include:

- Ease of Formatting: Customize fonts, colors, layouts, and styles.
- Collaboration Tools: Work on documents with others in real-time.
- Compatibility: Save documents in various formats (PDF, DOCX, etc.) for seamless sharing.

By the end of this chapter, you'll have a firm grasp of the basics of Microsoft Word, ready to start your first document.

## Installing and Opening Microsoft Word (Step-by-Step)

Step 1: Installing Microsoft Word

1. Go to the official Microsoft Office website: www.office.com.
2. Sign in with your Microsoft account. If you don't have one, create a free account.

3. Navigate to the "Install Office" button and select your preferred version (Microsoft 365 or standalone Word).
4. Follow the on-screen instructions to download and install the application.

Step 2: Opening Microsoft Word

1. Once installed, locate the Word application:
    o On Windows: Click the Start menu, type "Word," and select the app.
    o On macOS: Open Finder, navigate to Applications, and find "Microsoft Word."
2. Open Word, and you'll be greeted with the Start Page.

## Exploring the Word Interface

Understanding Word's interface is crucial to mastering the tool. Let's break it down into key sections:

### The Ribbon and Tabs

The Ribbon is the toolbar at the top of Word, divided into tabs like Home, Insert, and Layout. Each tab contains related tools:

- Home Tab: Formatting options (fonts, text alignment, styles).
- Insert Tab: Add tables, pictures, charts, and more.

- Layout Tab: Adjust margins, orientation, and spacing.

**The Quick Access Toolbar**

Located above the Ribbon, this toolbar provides shortcuts to commonly used commands like Save, Undo, and Redo.

- To customize it: Click the small dropdown arrow and select additional commands you want to add.

**The Status Bar**

At the bottom of the Word window, the Status Bar gives you real-time information about your document, including:

- Page number
- Word count
- Zoom level

Right-click the Status Bar to customize what's displayed.

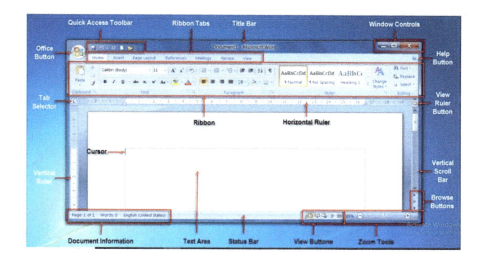

Summary

By now, you should understand:

1. How to install and open Microsoft Word.
2. The purpose of essential tools in the interface, like the Ribbon and Status Bar.
3. How to customize the Quick Access Toolbar.

13

# Chapter 2. Creating Your First Document

When you open Microsoft Word, you'll land on the Start Page. From here, starting a new document is easy:

Step 1: Starting a New Document

1. On the Start Page, click Blank Document to create a fresh document.
2. Alternatively, select a template (e.g., resumes, letters) by searching in the Search bar at the top. Templates come with preformatted designs to save time.

Step 2: Navigating Your New Document

1. Once the document opens, your cursor will blink in the top-left corner, ready for text input.
2. Start typing your content. Use the Enter key to create new paragraphs and the Tab key for indents.

# Saving Your Work: Save vs. Save As

Saving your document regularly is crucial to avoid losing your work. Microsoft Word provides two primary saving options:

## Save

- Use Save to update an existing document without changing its name or location.
- Shortcut: Press Ctrl + S (Windows) or Command + S (Mac).

## Save As

- Use Save As to save a copy of your document with a new name or in a different location.
- This is helpful if you're creating multiple versions of a file.

## Step-by-Step: How to Save

1. Click File in the Ribbon menu, then choose Save or Save As.

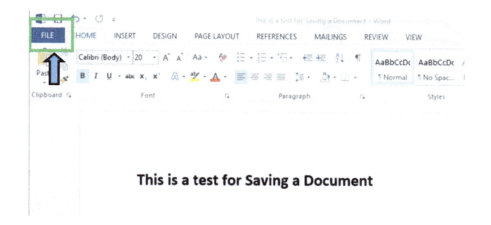

## This is a test for Saving a Document

2. For Save As, select the location where you want to save the file (e.g., your computer, OneDrive).

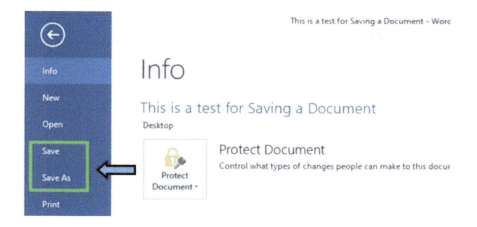

3. Enter a name for your document in the File Name field.
4. Click Save.

## File Formats (DOCX, PDF, etc.)

When saving your document, you can choose from various file formats depending on your needs:

1. DOCX: This is Word's default format, retaining all features like formatting and editing capabilities.
2. PDF: Ideal for sharing documents where formatting needs to remain consistent, even if the recipient doesn't have Word.
   - How to save as PDF:
     - Go to File > Save As.
     - Under the Save as type dropdown, select PDF.
3. RTF: A basic format compatible with many word processors.
4. TXT: Saves only plain text, stripping away formatting.

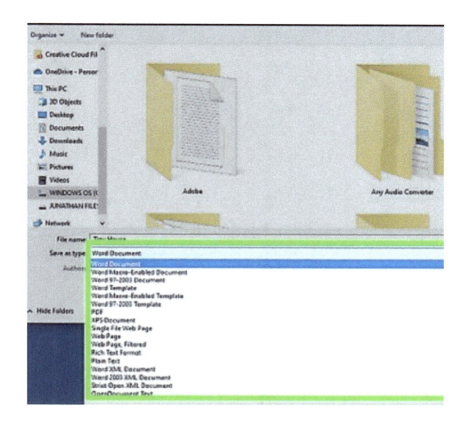

Summary

In this section, you've learned:

- How to start a blank document or use a template.
- The difference between Save and Save As, and when to use them.

The various file formats available in Microsoft Word and their use cases.

# Chapter 3. Formatting Basics

---

Formatting the text in your document is an essential part of making it look professional and easy to read. Let's start with how to change the font style, size, and color.

## Changing Font Style, Size, and Color

Step 1: Changing the Font Style

1. Select the text you want to change.
2. On the Home tab in the Font group, click the Font drop-down menu.
3. Choose a new font style from the list (e.g., Arial, Times New Roman, Calibri).

Step 2: Adjusting the Font Size

1. Select the text you want to resize.
2. In the Font group, click the Font Size drop-down menu.
3. Select a size (e.g., 12 pt, 14 pt) or type in a custom size.

Step 3: Changing the Font Color

1. Highlight the text.

2. Click on the Font Color button in the Font group (the letter A with a color bar under it).

3. Select a color from the palette, or click More Colors for custom options.

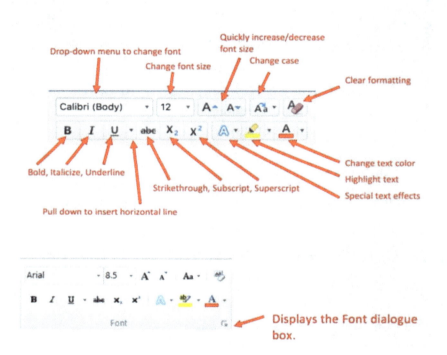

## Aligning Text (Left, Center, Right, Justify)

Text alignment helps organize your document and can improve readability. Word provides several alignment options:

Step 1: Left Alignment

- Left-align: This is the default setting for most documents. It aligns text along the left margin.
- To left-align, select the text and click the Align Left button in the Paragraph group on the Home tab (it looks like a set of horizontal lines aligned to the left).

Step 2: Center Alignment

- Center-align: This centers your text, which is commonly used for titles and headings.
- To center text, select it and click the Center button in the Paragraph group.

Step 3: Right Alignment

- Right-align: This aligns the text to the right margin, often used for dates or references in formal documents.
- To right-align, click the Align Right button in the Paragraph group.

Step 4: Justify Alignment

- Justify: This stretches your text so it's aligned on both the left and right margins, creating clean and even paragraphs.

- To justify, select the text and click the Justify button in the Paragraph group.

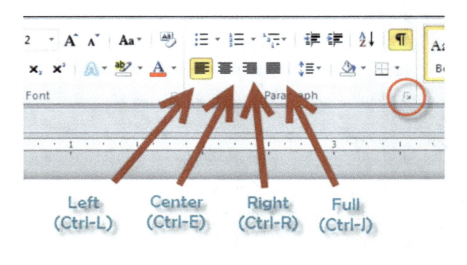

## Adding Bold, Italics, and Underlines

Bold, italics, and underlines are used to emphasize text. Here's how you can apply them to your document:

Step 1: Adding Bold

1. Highlight the text you want to make bold.
2. Click the Bold button in the Font group (it looks like a B).
   o Shortcut: Ctrl + B (Windows) or Command + B (Mac).

Step 2: Applying Italics

1. Highlight the text you want to italicize.
2. Click the Italic button in the Font group (it looks like an I).
   - Shortcut: Ctrl + I (Windows) or Command + I (Mac).

Step 3: Underlining Text

1. Select the text you want to underline.
2. Click the Underline button in the Font group (it looks like a U with a line under it).
   - Shortcut: Ctrl + U (Windows) or Command + U (Mac).

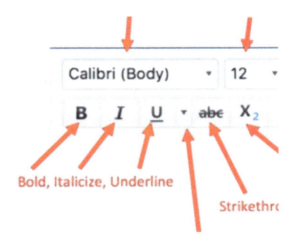

# Working with Text Spacing and Line Breaks

Proper text spacing can enhance readability and give your document a professional appearance. Let's explore text spacing and how to add line breaks.

Step 1: Adjusting Line Spacing

1. Select the text or paragraph you want to adjust.
2. Go to the Home tab, and in the Paragraph group, click the Line and Paragraph Spacing button.
3. Choose from preset options like 1.0 (single), 1.5, or 2.0 (double spacing).

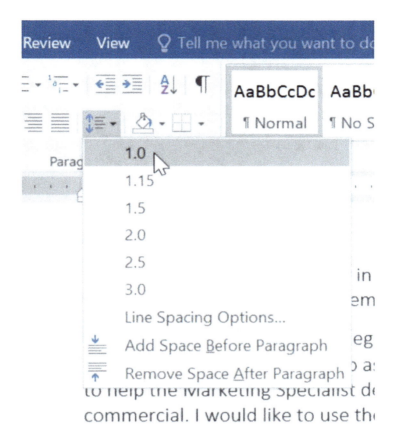

Step 2: Customizing Line Spacing

1. For more advanced options, click Line Spacing Options from the dropdown menu.
2. In the dialog box, adjust the Spacing Before and Spacing After settings to add more space between paragraphs.

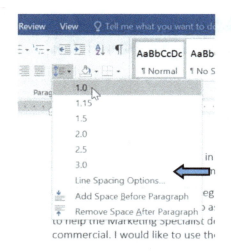

## Step 3: Inserting Line Breaks

A line break allows you to move to the next line without starting a new paragraph. This is useful for adding space between sections without creating extra paragraphs.

1. Place your cursor where you want the break.
2. Press Shift + Enter to insert a line break.

## Summary

In this section, you learned how to:

1. Change the font style, size, and color.
2. Align text to the left, center, right, or justify it.
3. Use bold, italics, and underlines for emphasis.

4. Adjust line spacing and insert line breaks for a clean and readable document.

# Chapter 4. Working with Paragraphs

Bullets and numbering are powerful tools for organizing information in a document. They make lists easier to follow and provide clarity, especially when you're outlining or detailing steps in a process.

## Using Bullets and Numbering

Step 1: Adding Bullets

1. Highlight the text you want to turn into a list.
2. Go to the Home tab and locate the Paragraph group.
3. Click on the Bullets button (it looks like three small dots).
   o This will convert your text into a bulleted list.

Step 2: Changing Bullet Style

1.  After clicking the Bullets button, click the small arrow next to it to open the Bullet Library.

2.  Choose from various bullet styles, including simple dots, arrows, check marks, or custom symbols.

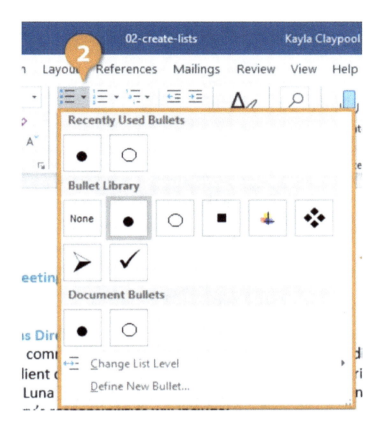

Step 3: Using Numbering

1. Highlight the text you want to number.
2. In the Paragraph group, click the Numbering button (it looks like a 1, 2, 3).
   ○ This will turn your selected text into a numbered list.
3. Like bullets, you can also customize the numbering format by clicking the small arrow next to the Numbering button

and selecting a style (e.g., 1, 2, 3, or i, ii, iii for Roman numerals).

Step 4: Customizing List Styles

1. You can change the bullet or numbering style anytime by selecting the list (i.e. the numbering) and then choosing a different option from the Bullets or Numbering menu.

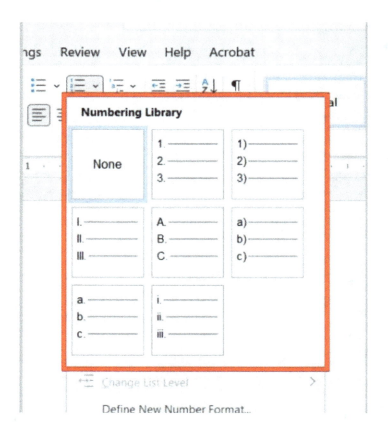

2. To adjust the list's indentation or spacing, use the Increase Indent and Decrease Indent buttons in the Paragraph group.

## Adjusting Line and Paragraph Spacing

Proper line and paragraph spacing is essential for making your document more readable and aesthetically pleasing. Let's review how to adjust the spacing:

Step 1: Adjusting Line Spacing

1. Highlight the text or paragraph you want to adjust.
2. Go to the Home tab and in the Paragraph group, click the Line and Paragraph Spacing button (it looks like a set of lines with arrows pointing up and down).
3. Select a preset option (e.g., 1.0 for single spacing, 1.5 for 1.5 spacing, or 2.0 for double spacing).

Step 2: Customizing Line Spacing

1. Click on Line Spacing Options from the dropdown menu to open the Paragraph dialog box.
2. Under the Spacing section, customize the Before and After settings.
   o Before: Adds space before the paragraph.
   o After: Adds space after the paragraph.

3. You can also adjust the Line Spacing to Exactly, At Least, or Multiple, depending on how you want the lines to be spaced.

Step 3: Adjusting Paragraph Spacing

1. Highlight the paragraph you want to adjust.
2. Follow the same steps above to adjust the spacing before and after the paragraph.
3. This ensures that your paragraphs are well-spaced and easy to read.

## Indenting Text (First Line and Hanging Indents)

Indentation helps to structure your document, especially for items like quotes, references, or lists. Let's learn how to use first-line and hanging indents.

Step 1: First-Line Indent

1. Place the cursor at the beginning of the paragraph you want to indent.
2. In the Paragraph group, click the Increase Indent button (it looks like an arrow pointing to the right).
3. Alternatively, press Tab on your keyboard to create a first-line indent.
   - This will move the first line of the paragraph to the right, leaving the rest of the paragraph aligned to the left.

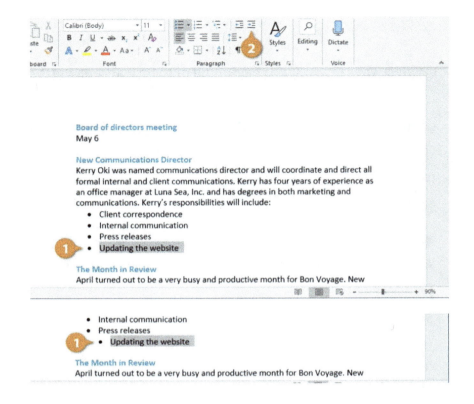

## Step 2: Hanging Indent

1. Select the paragraph you want to indent.
2. Go to the Home tab, then click the small arrow in the Paragraph group to open the Paragraph Settings dialog box.
3. Under Indentation, choose Hanging from the drop-down menu.
4. Set the By value (e.g., 0.5" for a standard indent).

- This will make the first line of the paragraph stay aligned with the left margin, and all subsequent lines will be indented.
- Hanging indents are commonly used for bibliographies or reference lists.

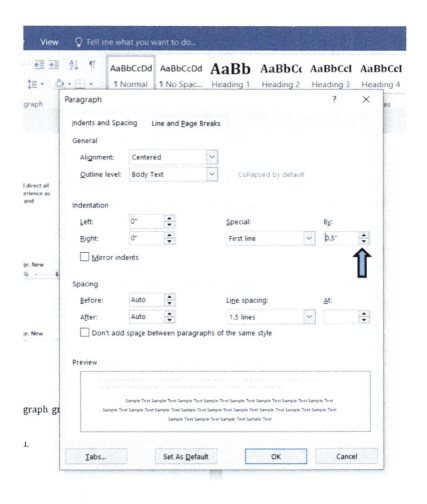

Summary

In this section, you learned:

- How to use bullets and numbering to organize information.
- How to adjust line and paragraph spacing for readability.
- How to use first-line and hanging indents to format your paragraphs.

# Chapter 5. Creating and Formatting Tables

Tables are incredibly useful for organizing data in rows and columns, whether you're making a schedule, budget, or list. Microsoft Word makes it easy to insert and customize tables to fit your needs. Here's how to get started.

## Inserting a Table

Step 1: Inserting a Table

1. Go to the Insert tab in the ribbon at the top of your screen.

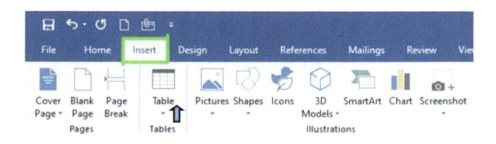

2. In the Tables group, click on the Table button. This will open a grid and allow you to select the number of rows and columns for your table.

   o Move your mouse over the grid to select the number of rows and columns you want, and click to insert the table.

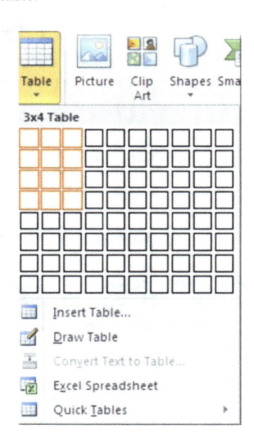

3. Alternatively, if you need more control over your table, select Insert Table from the dropdown menu. This opens a

dialog box where you can manually enter the number of columns and rows.

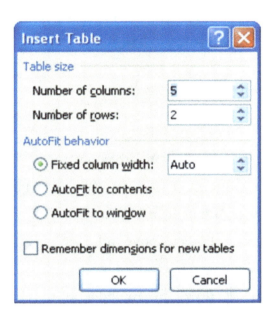

Step 2: Adjusting Table Size

1. Once your table is inserted, you can adjust its size by clicking and dragging the edges of the table or individual columns.
2. To adjust column width, hover your mouse over the vertical line between two columns, and when the cursor changes to a double arrow, click and drag to resize.

# Adding and Deleting Rows and Columns

As you work with your table, you may need to add or remove rows or columns to fit your content. Microsoft Word makes this process quick and easy.

Step 1: Adding Rows

1. Click anywhere inside the table.
2. Right-click on the row where you want to add a new row.
3. From the context menu, hover over Insert and select either Insert Rows Above or Insert Rows Below.
   - Insert Rows Above adds a new row above the selected row.
   - Insert Rows Below adds a new row below the selected row.

Step 2: Adding Columns

1. Click inside the table, then right-click on the column where you want to add a new one.
2. From the context menu, hover over Insert and select Insert Columns to the Left or Insert Columns to the Right.
   - This will add a new column on the left or right side of the selected column.

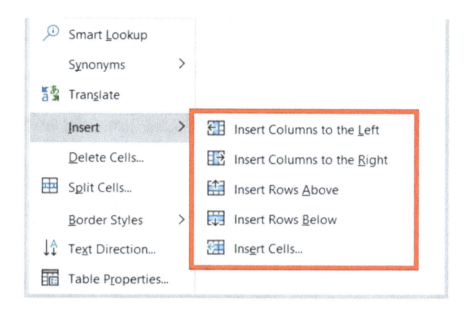

Step 3: Deleting Rows or Columns

1. To delete a row or column, right-click on the row or column you want to remove.
2. From the context menu, hover over Delete and choose either Delete Rows or Delete Columns.

## Merging and Splitting Cells

In tables, sometimes you may want to combine multiple cells into one large cell, or split a single cell into smaller parts. This is helpful when you need a heading that spans multiple columns or when you want to break up data.

Step 1: Merging Cells

1. Highlight the cells you want to merge (click and drag to select multiple cells).

2. Go to the Table Tools Design tab, located in the ribbon when the table is selected.

3. In the Merge group, click the Merge Cells button.

   o This combines the selected cells into a single larger cell.

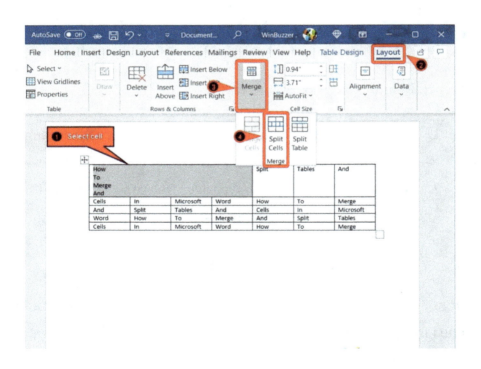

Step 2: Splitting Cells

1. Select the cell that you want to split.

2. Right-click and choose Split Cells from the context menu.

3. In the dialog box that appears, choose how many columns and rows you want to split the selected cell into.

   o For example, if you want to split one cell into two, set the Number of columns to 2.

4. Click OK, and the cell will be split into the selected number of smaller cells.

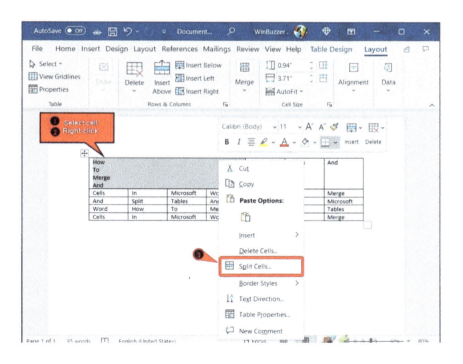

# Applying Table Styles

Once you've created your table, you can make it visually appealing by applying a predefined table style. Word provides many options to customize the look of your table.

Step 1: Applying a Predefined Style

1. Click anywhere inside the table to bring up the Table Tools Design tab in the ribbon.
2. In the Table Styles group, you'll see several style options to choose from.
   o Scroll through the options and click on the one you like. The style will be instantly applied to your table.

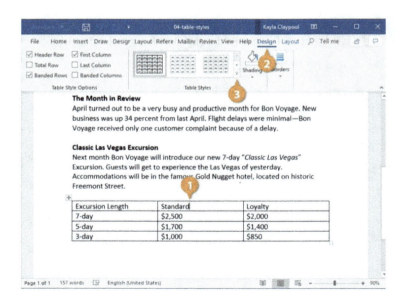

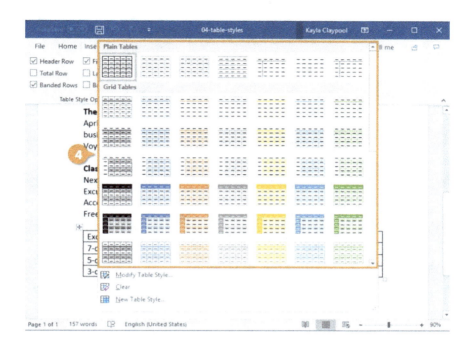

Step 2: Customizing Table Style

1. Once you've applied a style, you can further customize it.

2. To change the color of the table, click on the Shading button in the Table Styles group and choose a new color for the cells.

3. To change the border style, click on Borders and select from options like All Borders, Outside Borders, or Thick Box Border.

Step 3: Removing a Table Style

1. To remove a table style and revert to the default format, click on the Clear button in the Table Styles group.

2. This will remove all formatting from the table, giving you a blank slate to work with.

Summary

In this section, you've learned how to:

- Insert a table and adjust its size.
- Add and delete rows and columns to modify your table layout.
- Merge and split cells to customize the structure of your table.
- Apply and customize table styles for a more visually appealing table.

# Chapter 6. Inserting Visual Elements

In this section, we will cover how to insert various visual elements to enhance your document. Visuals like images, shapes, icons, and text boxes can make your document more engaging and help convey information more clearly. Follow these simple steps to incorporate visual elements into your document!

## Adding Images and Screenshots to Documents

Images are a great way to illustrate concepts and add appeal to your documents. Whether you're adding a picture from your computer or a screenshot, Word makes it simple to insert visuals into your work.

Step 1: Inserting an Image from Your Computer

1. Place your cursor where you want the image to appear in the document.
2. Go to the Insert tab on the ribbon.

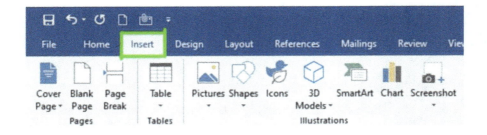

3. In the Illustrations group, click on Pictures.

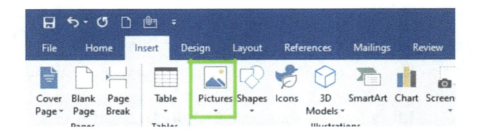

4. From the dropdown menu, select This Device.

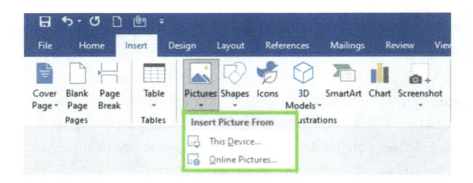

5. A file explorer window will open. Navigate to the image you want to insert, select it, and click Insert.
   o The image will now appear in your document.

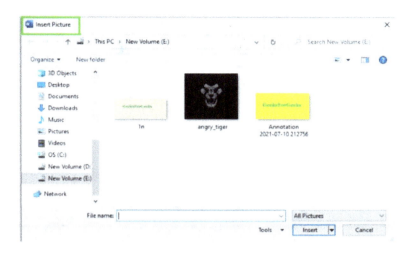

## Step 2: Inserting a Screenshot

1. Place your cursor in the spot where you want the screenshot.
2. On the Insert tab, click Screenshot in the Illustrations group.
3. Word will display all open windows as thumbnail previews. Choose the window from which you want to capture the screenshot.
4. Once you click on the window, Word will automatically insert a screenshot of that window into your document.
   - If you want to capture a part of the screen, click Screen Clipping instead, and select the area you want to capture.

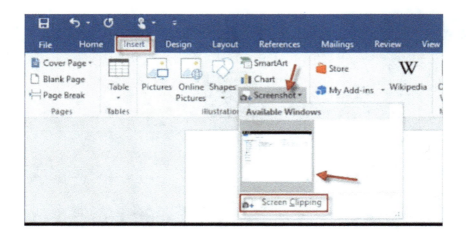

Step 3: Adjusting the Image

1. After inserting an image, you can resize it by clicking and dragging the corner handles.
   - Hold the Shift key while resizing to maintain the image's proportions.
2. To move the image, click on it and drag it to a new position in the document.

## Using Shapes, Icons, and SmartArt

Microsoft Word also allows you to add shapes, icons, and SmartArt to make your document visually appealing and more organized. These features are especially useful for creating infographics, process flows, or just adding simple design elements.

Step 1: Inserting Shapes

1. Place your cursor where you want to insert a shape.
2. On the Insert tab, click Shapes in the Illustrations group.

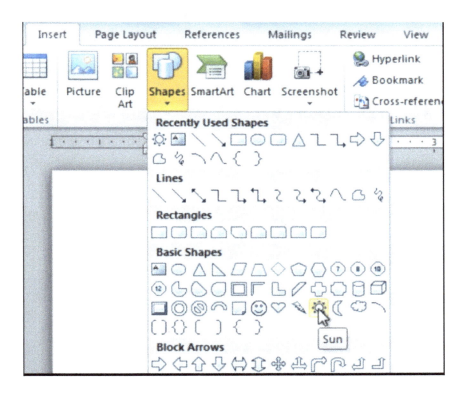

3. From the dropdown menu, select the shape you want to insert (such as a rectangle, circle, or arrow).
4. Click and drag to draw the shape. You can adjust the size by clicking and dragging the corners.

5. To change the shape's color, select the shape and go to the Format tab. In the Shape Styles group, you can pick a fill color, border color, and even add effects like shadows.

Step 2: Inserting Icons

1. Place your cursor where you want the icon to appear.
2. On the Insert tab, click Icons in the Illustrations group.
3. A library of icons will open. Browse through the available categories or use the search bar to find the icon you need.
4. Once you find the right icon, click on it and select Insert.
   - The icon will appear in your document, and you can resize and adjust it just like any other shape.

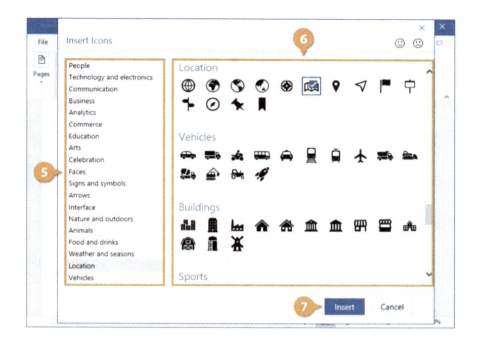

Step 3: Inserting SmartArt

1. Place your cursor where you want to insert a SmartArt graphic.

2. On the Insert tab, click SmartArt in the Illustrations group.

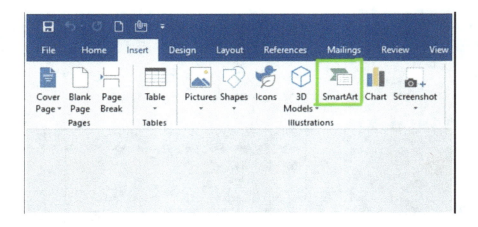

3. A window will open with various SmartArt graphic styles (like lists, processes, or hierarchies).

4. Select the style that fits your needs, and click OK.

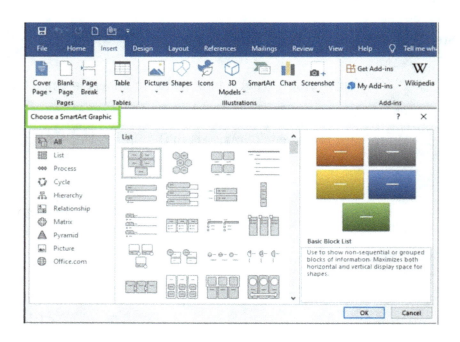

5. You can now add text to the SmartArt. Click on the placeholders within the graphic and type your text.
6. To modify the design or color scheme of the SmartArt, use the SmartArt Tools Design and Format tabs in the ribbon.

## Working with Text Boxes

Text boxes are useful for adding text in specific locations within a document. Whether you're creating a sidebar, a quote box, or a callout, text boxes provide flexibility in positioning text.

Step 1: Inserting a Text Box

1. Place your cursor where you want the text box to appear.
2. On the Insert tab, click Text Box in the Text group.
3. You can choose from several predefined text box styles, or click Simple Text Box to create a plain one.
4. A text box will appear in your document. You can move it by clicking and dragging it, or resize it by clicking and dragging the corners.
5. Type the text you want inside the text box.

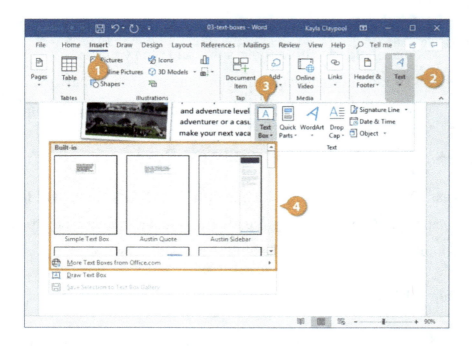

Step 2: Formatting the Text Box

1.  Once your text box is selected, go to the Format tab in the ribbon.

2.  In the Text Box Styles group, you can adjust the fill color, outline, and add effects like shadows or reflections.

3.  You can also adjust the text inside the box by changing the font, size, color, and alignment, just like with regular text.

Step 3: Removing a Text Box

1. To remove a text box, click on it to select it.
2. Press Delete on your keyboard, or right-click and select Cut from the context menu.

Summary

In this section, you've learned how to:

- Add images and screenshots to your document for better illustration.

- Use shapes, icons, and SmartArt to create visually appealing and informative graphics.
- Insert and format text boxes for more control over the placement of your text.

# Chapter 7. Page Layout and Design

In this section, we will dive into how to adjust the layout of your document to make it look professional and organized. We'll cover how to set up margins, choose the correct page size and orientation, add headers and footers, and use section and page breaks to structure your document. Follow along with the steps below to create a polished, well-structured document.

## Setting Margins, Page Orientation, and Size

Page layout is essential for controlling how your document appears when printed or viewed on a screen. Microsoft Word allows you to customize the margins, page orientation, and size to suit the type of document you're working on.

Step 1: Setting Margins

1. Go to the Layout tab in the ribbon.
2. In the Page Setup group, click Margins.

3. A dropdown menu will appear with several predefined margin options, such as Normal, Narrow, Wide, and Custom Margins.

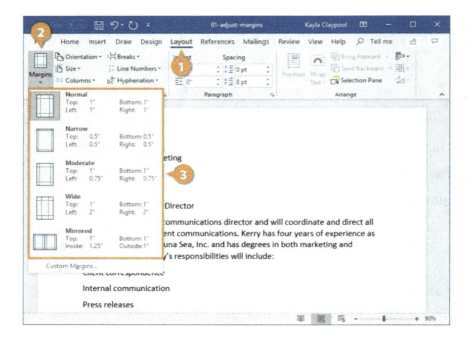

4. Select the margin option that fits your needs. If you want to set custom margins, click on Custom Margins at the bottom of the list. This will open the Page Setup dialog box, where you can adjust the Top, Bottom, Left, and Right margins.
5. Click OK to apply your chosen margins.

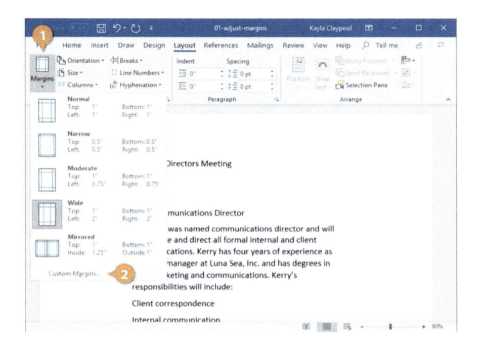

responsibilities will include:

Client correspondence

Internal communication

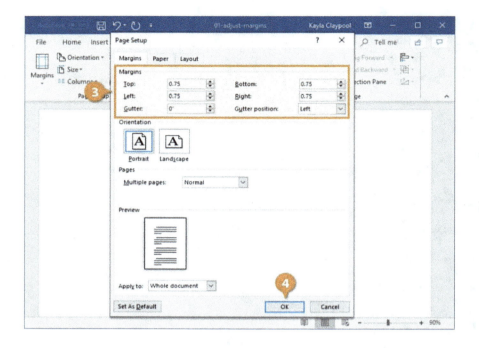

Step 2: Setting Page Orientation

1. In the Layout tab, click Orientation in the Page Setup group.

2. You'll have two options: Portrait (vertical) and Landscape (horizontal). Select the one that best suits your document's layout.

3. The page orientation will immediately change for your document.

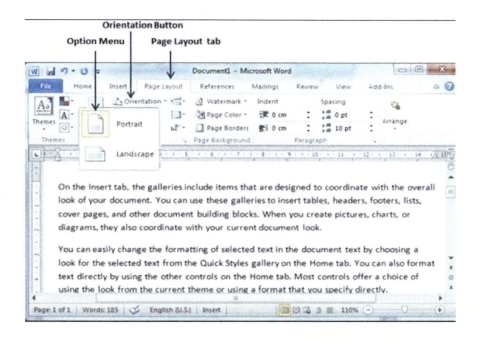

Step 3: Setting Page Size

1. In the Layout tab, click Size in the Page Setup group.
2. A list of common page sizes will appear (such as Letter, A4, etc.). Select the size that fits your needs.
3. If you need a custom page size, click More Paper Sizes at the bottom of the list. This opens the Page Setup dialog box, where you can input your custom width and height.

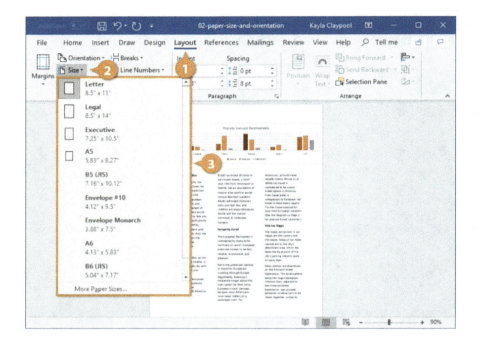

## Adding Headers, Footers, and Page Numbers

Headers and footers are areas where you can add information that you want to appear on every page of your document, such as a title, author name, or page numbers. Let's go step-by-step on how to add and customize these elements.

Step 1: Inserting a Header

1. Go to the Insert tab on the ribbon.

2. In the Header & Footer group, click Header.

3. You'll see several predefined header styles to choose from. Select one that suits your document, or click Edit Header to create a custom header.

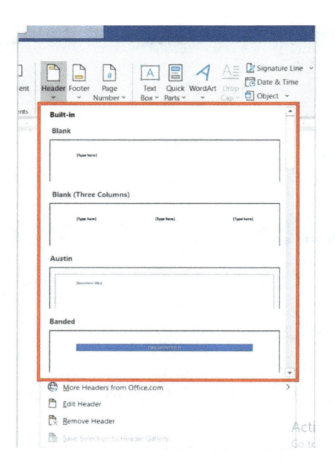

4. After selecting a header, you can type or insert elements like the document title, author name, or company logo.

5. Once you're done, click Close Header and Footer in the ribbon to return to the body of the document.

Step 2: Inserting a Footer

1. Go to the Insert tab again.
2. In the Header & Footer group, click Footer.
3. Select one of the predefined footer styles, or click Edit Footer for a custom footer.
4. Add the information you want to appear at the bottom of each page, such as page numbers or document details (e.g., confidentiality notice).
5. Click Close Header and Footer to finish.

Step 3: Adding Page Numbers

1. With the footer or header section active, go to the Insert tab.

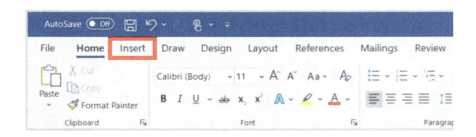

2. Click Page Number in the Header & Footer group.

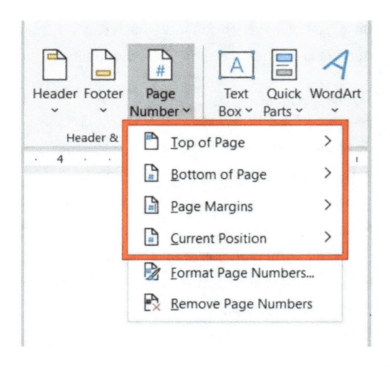

3. Choose where you want the page number to appear: Top of Page, Bottom of Page, or Current Position.

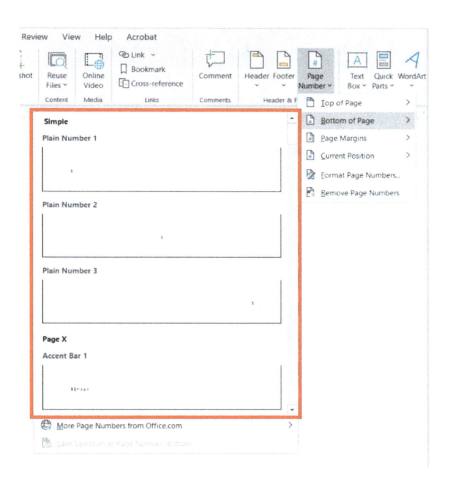

4. You can also format the page numbers to display in different styles (e.g., 1, 2, 3, or i, ii, iii) by selecting Format Page Numbers.

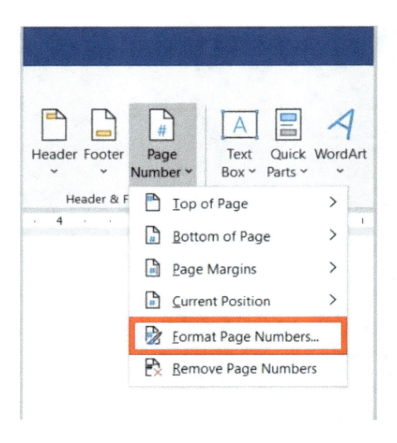

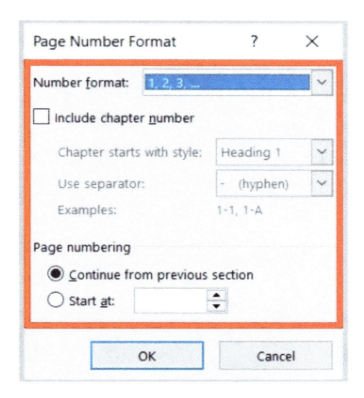

5. If you only want page numbers to appear starting from a specific page (e.g., excluding the cover page), use the Different First Page option in the Header & Footer tab.

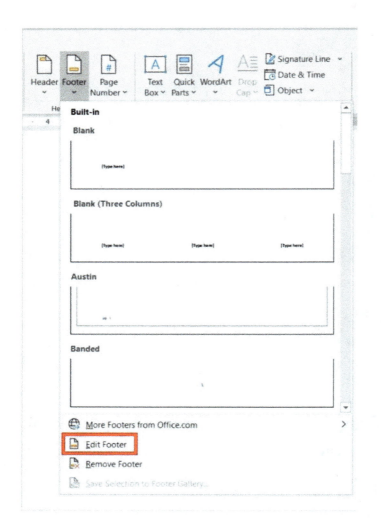

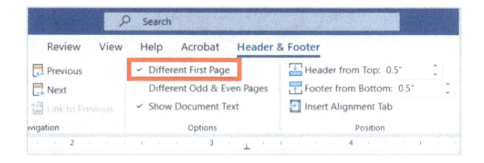

## Inserting Section and Page Breaks

Section breaks and page breaks are useful tools when you need to divide your document into different sections, each with its own formatting (such as different headers/footers, page numbering, or margins). Here's how you can insert and work with breaks.

Step 1: Inserting a Page Break

1. Place your cursor where you want to start a new page.
2. Go to the Insert tab.
3. In the Pages group, click Page Break.
4. Word will automatically start a new page from where your cursor was.

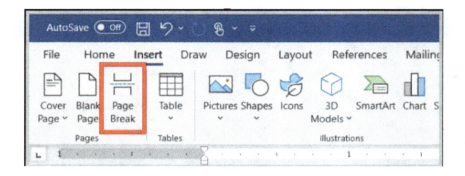

Step 2: Inserting a Section Break

1. Place your cursor where you want the section to begin.
2. Go to the Layout tab.

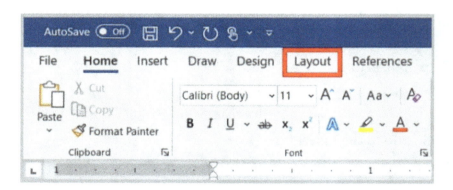

3. In the Page Setup group, click Breaks.

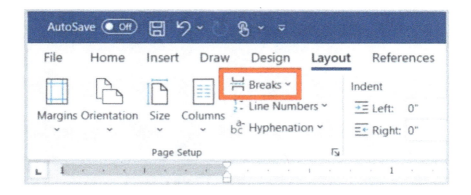

4. From the dropdown menu, you will see several types of section breaks:

   o  Next Page: Starts a new section on the next page.

   o  Continuous: Starts a new section on the same page.

   o  Even Page or Odd Page: Starts a new section on the next even or odd page.

5. Select the appropriate break for your document.

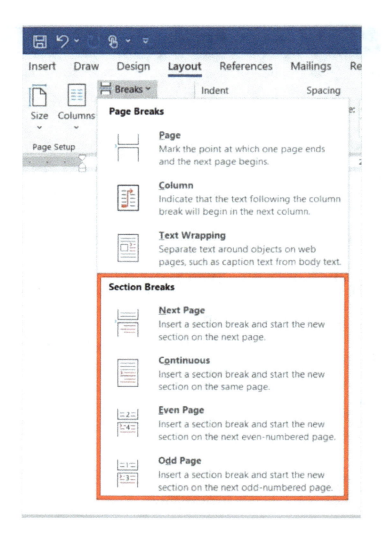

Step 3: Customizing Sections After Inserting Breaks

- After inserting a section break, you can customize each section's layout independently. This allows you to change things like page numbering, headers, or footers for different sections of your document.

- For example, to create different page numbering for each section, go to the Header & Footer tab and unlink the sections by clicking Link to Previous. Then, you can insert new page numbers specific to the section.

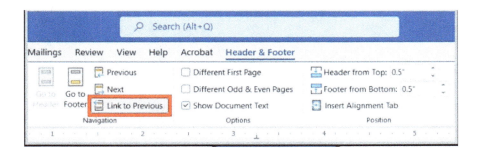

Summary

In this section, you've learned how to:

- Set the margins, page size, and orientation for your document to fit your needs.
- Add headers, footers, and page numbers for a professional look and consistent navigation throughout the document.
- Insert section and page breaks to divide your document into manageable, well-formatted sections.

# Chapter 8. Proofing and Reviewing Tools

Proofing and reviewing your document are essential steps to ensure your content is clear, accurate, and polished. Microsoft Word provides a set of tools that help you spot spelling and grammatical errors, improve your word choice, track the length of your document, and even collaborate with others through comments. In this section, we will explore how to use these tools effectively.

## Using Spelling and Grammar Check

One of the most fundamental proofing tools in Microsoft Word is the Spelling and Grammar check. This feature helps you identify errors in your writing and provides suggestions to correct them. Here's how you can run a spell check in Word:

Step 1: Running a Spelling and Grammar Check Automatically

1. Word automatically checks your spelling and grammar as you type. Misspelled words will be underlined in red, and grammatical issues will be underlined in blue.

2. To fix an issue, simply right-click on the underlined word. A menu will appear with suggestions. You can click the correct suggestion to replace the word.

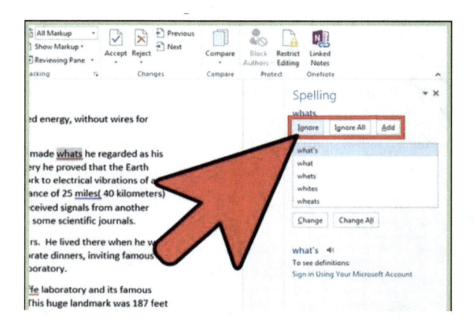

3. If Word doesn't provide a suggestion, you can choose Ignore, Ignore All, or Add to Dictionary if the word is correct but not in the dictionary.

Step 2: Manually Running Spelling and Grammar Check

1. Go to the Review tab in the ribbon.
2. In the Proofing group, click on Spelling & Grammar.

3. A dialog box will appear, starting the check at the beginning of your document. Word will highlight each issue, and you can choose to Ignore, Change, or Change All.

4. Click OK to complete the check once all errors have been addressed.

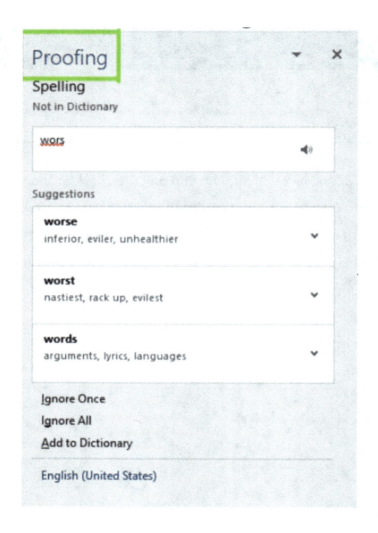

Step 3: Customizing Spelling and Grammar Check Settings

1. Go to File > Options to open the Word Options dialog.
2. Select Proofing in the left pane.

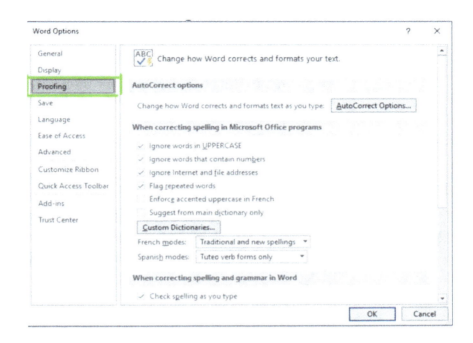

3. Under When correcting spelling and grammar in Word, you can customize what Word checks, including grammar rules, formatting, and more. You can turn off or on various rules for better control over how Word helps you proofread your content.

## Thesaurus and Word Count

Sometimes, you may want to find better words to express your ideas or check the length of your document. Microsoft Word offers tools like the Thesaurus and Word Count to help with these tasks.

Step 1: Using the Thesaurus

1. To use the Thesaurus, right-click on any word in your document that you want to find synonyms for.
2. From the context menu, select Synonyms and then choose Thesaurus.

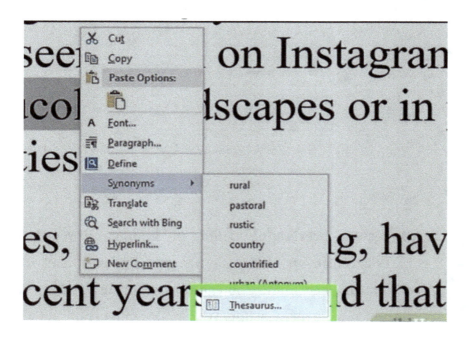

3. The Research pane will open, showing you a list of synonyms for the selected word.
4. You can click on any synonym to replace the word in your document. If you want more options, click Show All to explore additional alternatives.

Pro Tip: You can also use the shortcut Shift + F7 to quickly open the Thesaurus.

Step 2: Checking Word Count

1. To check the word count of your document, go to the Review tab.
2. In the Proofing group, click Word Count.
3. The Word Count dialog box will open, showing statistics such as:
   o Total words
   o Character count (with and without spaces)
   o Paragraph count
   o Line count
   o And more
4. You can choose to include or exclude textboxes, footnotes, and endnotes by checking or unchecking the box in the dialog box.

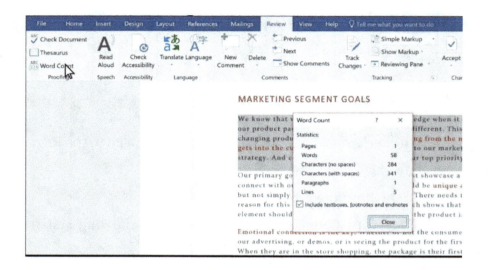

MARKETING SEGMENT GOALS

## Adding and Managing Comments

If you're collaborating with others or reviewing your own work, comments can be an essential tool to highlight areas that need improvement or to leave notes for later. In this section, we'll explore how to add, view, and manage comments in your document.

Step 1: Adding Comments

1.  Select the text or area of the document where you want to add a comment.
2.  Go to the Review tab in the ribbon.
3.  In the Comments group, click New Comment.

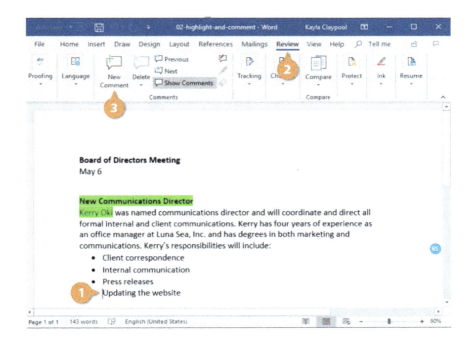

4. A comment box will appear on the right side of your document. Type your comment inside the box.

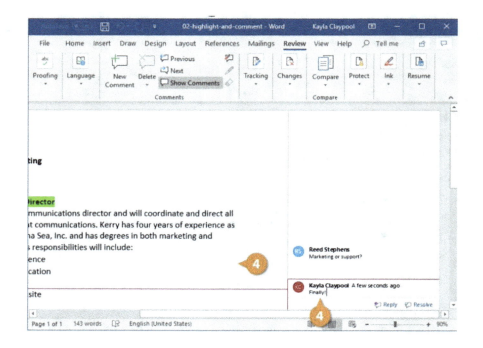

5. If you need to add more comments, simply click on the part of the document where you want to comment, and repeat the steps.

Step 2: Managing Comments

- Editing a Comment: Click on an existing comment and modify its text directly in the comment box.
- Deleting a Comment: Right-click on the comment and choose Delete Comment or click Delete in the Comments group to remove it.

- Navigating Through Comments: To quickly navigate between comments, use the Previous and Next buttons in the Comments group under the Review tab.

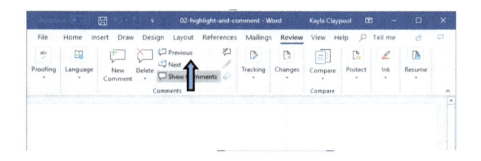

- Replying to Comments: If you're working with others, you can reply to a comment by clicking Reply inside the comment box.

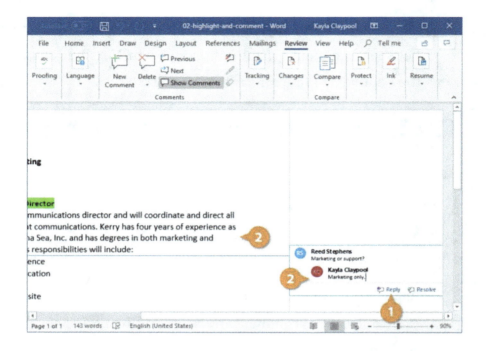

Step 3: Reviewing and Finalizing Comments

- If you're done with reviewing, you can choose to delete all comments in the document. To do this, go to the Review tab, click Delete in the Comments group, and select Delete All Comments in Document.

Summary

In this section, you've learned how to:

- Use Spelling and Grammar Check to catch errors and improve the quality of your writing.
- Utilize the Thesaurus to find better word choices and expand your vocabulary.
- Check your Word Count to ensure your document meets length requirements.
- Add and manage comments for collaboration or personal notes.

# Chapter 9. Collaboration and Sharing

I n today's digital world, collaboration is key, especially when working on documents with others. Microsoft Word offers several features that make sharing and reviewing documents easy and efficient. Whether you're working on a team project, reviewing a draft, or simply sending a file for feedback, Word provides powerful tools to track changes, leave comments, and share documents with ease.

In this section, we'll explore how to use these tools to collaborate and share your work seamlessly.

## Tracking Changes and Accepting/Rejecting Edits

When collaborating on a document, it's important to track the changes made by others so that you can review and decide whether to accept or reject them. Microsoft Word makes this process easy through its Track Changes feature.

Step 1: Turning on Track Changes

1. Open your document in Word.

2. Go to the Review tab in the ribbon.

3. In the Tracking group, click Track Changes. This will highlight any changes made to the document, such as insertions, deletions, and formatting changes.

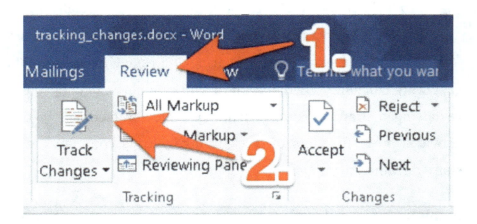

4. You can choose to track changes for all edits or customize it by selecting Track Changes Options to choose how you want the changes to be displayed (e.g., color, underline, strikethrough).

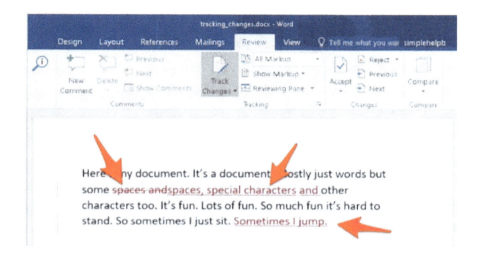

## Step 2: Viewing and Accepting/Rejecting Edits

1. After turning on Track Changes, any changes made by collaborators will appear in the document. Inserted text is underlined, while deleted text is crossed out.

2. To accept or reject a change, go to the Review tab and find the Changes group.

3. Use the Accept or Reject buttons to manage each change:

   o Accept: Click to accept the change and incorporate it into the document.

   o Reject: Click to reject the change and revert to the original content.

4. You can also use Accept All or Reject All if you want to accept or reject all changes in the document at once.

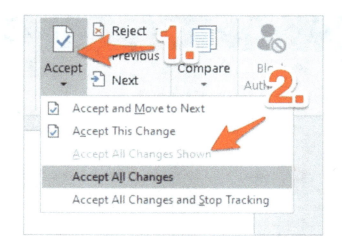

## Adding Comments and Resolving Feedback

Comments are an essential part of collaboration, as they allow you to give and receive feedback without altering the document itself. Let's dive into how you can use comments to communicate with collaborators and how to resolve feedback.

Step 1: Adding Comments

1. Select the text or area where you want to add a comment.
2. Go to the Review tab.
3. Click New Comment in the Comments group.

4. Type your comment in the comment box that appears in the right margin.

5. If you need to add more comments, just repeat this process.

Step 2: Resolving and Managing Comments

1. Once a comment has been addressed, you can mark it as Resolved. To do this, simply click on the comment and select Resolve from the options that appear.

2. If you want to delete a comment, right-click on the comment and choose Delete. You can delete a single comment or choose Delete All Comments in Document to remove them all at once.

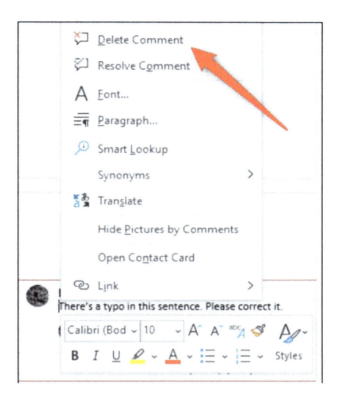

3. To navigate between comments, use the Previous and Next buttons in the Comments group.

Step 3: Viewing Comments in a Review Pane

1. To view all comments at once, click Reviewing Pane in the Tracking group. This opens a pane on the left where all the comments and changes are listed in chronological order.
2. You can click on any comment in the Reviewing Pane to jump directly to that section of the document.

# Sharing Documents via OneDrive or Email

Sharing your document with others for feedback or collaboration is easy with Microsoft Word. You can either use OneDrive for real-time collaboration or send your document via email.

Step 1: Sharing via OneDrive

1.  To start, make sure your document is saved to OneDrive (Microsoft's cloud storage). If you haven't done so already, save your file by selecting File > Save As and choose OneDrive as the destination.

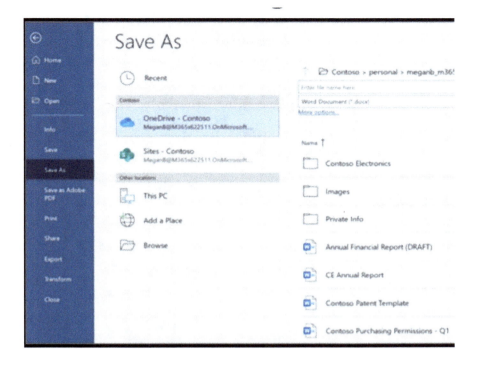

2. Once saved to OneDrive, go to the File tab, select Share, and click on Invite People.

3. You can enter the email addresses of people you want to share the document with. Choose whether you want them to be able to Edit or View the document.

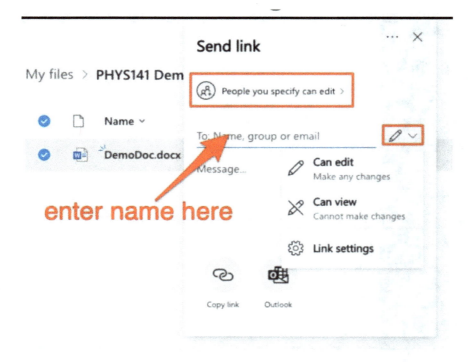

4. Click Share, and the recipients will receive an email with a link to your document.

Step 2: Sharing via Email

1. If you prefer to share your document directly via email, go to the File tab, select Share, and choose Email.

2. You can choose to send the document as an Attachment or Send as PDF.

3. After selecting your preferred option, Word will open your email client, and you can send the document directly to the recipient.

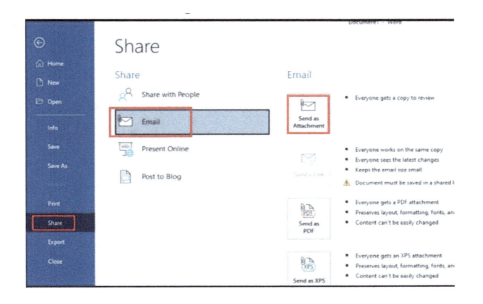

## Real-Time Collaboration View

Microsoft Word allows you to collaborate with others in real-time, meaning that multiple users can edit the same document simultaneously. This feature is especially useful when working in teams or during group projects. The changes made by others will appear immediately, and you can even see who is working on what section.

Step 1: Enabling Real-Time Collaboration

1. To enable real-time collaboration, you need to save your document to OneDrive, as mentioned earlier.
2. Once saved, click the Share button in the File tab and invite others to edit the document.
3. As others join, their initials will appear in the top right corner of the screen. You will be able to see their changes in real-time, and they will be able to see yours.
4. If someone else is editing a section of the document, Word will highlight that area with their name, making it clear who is working on what.

Step 2: Commenting During Collaboration

1. In real-time collaboration, you can also leave comments for others by selecting text and clicking New Comment in the Review tab.
2. All participants will be able to see and respond to the comments in real time.

Summary

In this section, you've learned how to:

- Track changes and manage edits made by collaborators.

- Add and manage comments to provide feedback and resolve issues.
- Share documents via OneDrive for real-time collaboration or email for quick distribution.
- Collaborate in real-time, making edits and reviewing documents as a team.

# Chapter 10. Printing and Exporting Documents

After all your hard work in creating and formatting your document, the final step often involves sharing it in physical or digital form. Microsoft Word provides straightforward tools to print your document or export it as a PDF for easy sharing. In this section, we'll explore how to set up your print options, preview your document before printing, and export it as a PDF.

Let's walk through these options step-by-step so you can confidently manage how your document looks when it leaves Word.

Setting Up Print Options

When you're ready to print your document, it's important to customize your print settings to ensure that everything prints as expected. Microsoft Word gives you several options to control how your document is printed.

Step 1: Open the Print Menu

1. Click on the File tab in the ribbon.

2. From the drop-down menu, click Print. This will open the Print window where you can adjust all of your printing options.

Step 2: Selecting a Printer

1. At the top of the Print window, you'll see a dropdown list of available printers. Make sure the correct printer is selected. If you have multiple printers connected to your computer (e.g., local or network printers), choose the one you want to use.

Step 3: Choosing Number of Copies

1. Under the printer selection, you can set how many copies of your document you wish to print.
2. Simply change the Copies field to the desired number.

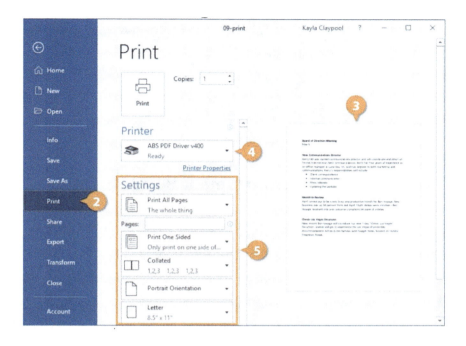

Step 4: Page Range

1. If you only want to print certain pages of your document, you can specify a Page Range.

   ○ All Pages: Prints the entire document.

   ○ Pages: Allows you to type in specific pages you want to print (e.g., pages 1, 3, and 5).

   ○ Current Page: Prints only the page you're currently viewing.

Step 5: Adjusting Print Settings

1. Click on Printer Properties or Preferences to adjust the printer's settings, such as:
   - Paper size (A4, letter, etc.)
   - Orientation (portrait or landscape)
   - Quality settings (draft, normal, high quality)

## Previewing Your Document Before Printing

Before you send your document to the printer, it's essential to preview it to ensure that everything looks right—this includes checking for page breaks, margins, and overall layout. Word offers a Print Preview feature that allows you to see how your document will appear once printed.

Step 1: Open Print Preview

1. After clicking File > Print, the Print Preview window will appear on the right side.
2. In this view, you can see how each page of your document will look when printed.

Step 2: Navigating the Pages

1. If your document is more than one page, you can use the Next and Previous buttons at the bottom of the preview to navigate through all the pages.

2. This will give you a sense of how the content flows across pages and allow you to spot any formatting issues.

Step 3: Zoom In and Out

1. To get a closer look at specific sections, use the zoom controls at the bottom-right corner of the preview window.
2. This can help you make sure things like headers, footers, and page numbers are correctly placed.

Step 4: Adjusting Margins and Layouts

1. If you see that your document is not laid out the way you want it, go back to the main document and adjust the margins or layout. You can do this under the Layout tab in the ribbon, where you can change page orientation or set custom margins.

## Exporting as PDF

Sometimes, you may need to share your document digitally or ensure that the formatting stays consistent regardless of where it's opened. This is where exporting as a PDF comes in handy. PDF files are universally compatible and preserve the layout, fonts, and images exactly as they appear in the document.

Step 1: Exporting the Document

1. Click on the File tab and select Save As.
2. In the Save As window, choose the location where you want to save the file (e.g., your desktop or a folder).
3. From the dropdown menu under the Save as type field, select PDF.

Step 2: Adjusting PDF Settings

1. After selecting PDF, you have a few options:
   o Standard: Best for documents that need to be printed.
   o Minimum size: Compresses the document for email or web use.
2. Click Options if you need more customization (e.g., selecting which pages to export, excluding document properties, etc.).

Step 3: Saving the PDF

1. After making your selections, click Save.
2. The document will be saved as a PDF in the location you specified, and it will be ready to share.

Summary

In this section, we covered how to:

- Set up print options including selecting a printer, adjusting the page range, and choosing the number of copies.
- Preview your document before printing to ensure that everything is formatted correctly.
- Export your document as a PDF to preserve formatting and make it easier to share digitally.

# Part 2: Microsoft Excel for Beginners

# Chapter 11. Getting Started with Microsoft Excel

Microsoft Excel is one of the most powerful and widely used tools for working with numbers, data, and analysis. Whether you're managing a budget, creating reports, or analyzing trends, Excel offers a flexible and user-friendly platform for organizing information in an effective way. In this section, we'll explore the basics of Microsoft Excel—what it is, why it's so important, how to install it, and how to navigate its interface.

Let's get started!

## Introduction to Excel: What It's For and Key Benefits

Microsoft Excel is a spreadsheet software that helps users organize, analyze, and visualize data. Unlike simple text editors, Excel provides features for working with rows and columns, performing calculations, and creating visual charts and graphs.

**Key Benefits of Excel:**

- Data Organization: Excel's grid system allows you to input and manage large amounts of data in a structured way.
- Formulas and Functions: You can use formulas and built-in functions to perform complex calculations automatically.
- Data Analysis: Excel enables you to analyze data with tools like pivot tables, filters, and sorting options.
- Visualization: It allows for the creation of various charts and graphs to visually represent data, making it easier to understand.
- Collaboration: Excel integrates with cloud services like OneDrive, enabling real-time collaboration on documents.

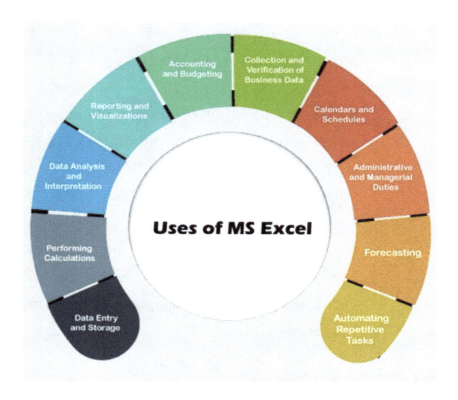

## Installing and Opening Microsoft Excel

Before you can begin using Excel, you need to have it installed on your device. Here's a step-by-step guide on how to install and open Microsoft Excel.

Step 1: Installing Microsoft Excel

1. Using Microsoft 365 Subscription:

- o If you have a Microsoft 365 subscription, go to https://www.office.com and sign in with your Microsoft account.
- o Click on the Install Office button and follow the on-screen instructions to download and install the Office suite, including Excel.
2. Using Office Home & Student Edition:
   - o If you purchased a one-time copy of Microsoft Office (such as Office Home & Student), enter the product key you received, and download the installer.
   - o Follow the installation prompts to install Excel on your device.

Step 2: Opening Microsoft Excel

1. Once Excel is installed, you can open it in a couple of ways:
   - o Windows: Click the Start Menu and search for Microsoft Excel. Click the Excel icon to open it.
   - o Mac: Open Finder, go to the Applications folder, and click on Microsoft Excel.
   - o From Office Online: If you're using Microsoft 365 online, go to https://www.office.com and select Excel from the apps list.

# Exploring the Excel Interface

The Excel interface is designed to be easy to use, with several sections that you'll need to become familiar with in order to work effectively. Let's take a closer look at these areas, step by step.

## The Ribbon, Tabs, and Quick Access Toolbar

When you open Excel, the first thing you'll notice is the Ribbon at the top of the screen. This contains all the tools and commands you'll use to work in Excel. The Ribbon is divided into several tabs (e.g., Home, Insert, Page Layout), each containing specific groups of commands.

Step 1: Understanding the Ribbon

- The Home Tab is where you'll find the most frequently used commands, like formatting, copy/paste, alignment, and basic cell operations.
- The Insert Tab is where you can add charts, tables, pictures, and other objects.
- Each tab is further divided into groups. For example, under the Home tab, the Font group allows you to change the font type, size, and color of text.

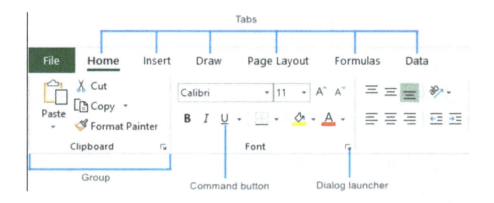

Step 2: Quick Access Toolbar

- The Quick Access Toolbar sits at the very top of the Excel window, above the Ribbon. It allows you to add your most commonly used commands for easy access.

- You can customize this toolbar by clicking the small down arrow to the right and selecting commands you use often, such as Save, Undo, and Redo.

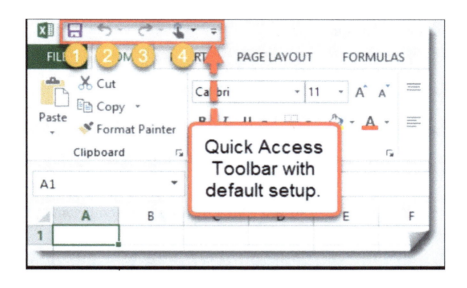

## The Formula Bar and Status Bar

As you enter data into Excel, you'll use two key areas: the Formula Bar and the Status Bar. These two sections display important information and offer additional controls to work with data in your spreadsheet.

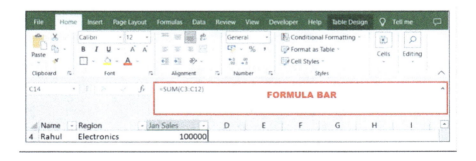

Step 1: The Formula Bar

- The Formula Bar is located just above the worksheet, and it's where you can see and edit the content of the selected cell.
- When you click on a cell in the spreadsheet, the contents of that cell (whether a number, text, or formula) will appear in the Formula Bar.
- You can also type a formula directly into the Formula Bar, which Excel will then apply to the selected cell.

Step 2: The Status Bar

- The Status Bar is located at the bottom of the Excel window. It provides important information about your document, such as:
  - The current page number when you're working with a multi-page document.
  - Cell information like the sum, average, or count of the selected range.
  - Zoom slider: Allows you to zoom in and out of your spreadsheet view.

Excel Status Bar

Cell mode     Accessibility check     Workbook views     Zoom slider

## Summary

In this section, we:

- Explored what Microsoft Excel is, its key benefits, and how it can help you with data analysis, budgeting, and more.
- Learned how to install and open Microsoft Excel, whether you're using a Microsoft 365 subscription or the one-time purchase version.

Walked through the Excel interface, familiarizing you with the Ribbon, Tabs, Quick Access Toolbar, Formula Bar, and Status Bar.

# Chapter 12. Creating Your First Spreadsheet

N ow that you're familiar with the Excel interface, it's time to create your first spreadsheet. Spreadsheets are essentially workbooks that contain worksheets (which are individual pages where you enter your data). In this section, we'll guide you through the process of creating a new workbook, saving your work, and understanding how sheets are organized.

Let's get started with the basics of creating a spreadsheet!

## Starting a New Workbook

Step 1: Opening Excel

- To start a new workbook, open Microsoft Excel as discussed in the previous section. Once Excel is open, you'll be greeted with a blank workbook or the Excel start screen.

Step 2: Creating a New Workbook

- From the Start Screen:

o   When you open Excel, you'll usually see the New tab selected. Here you can click on Blank Workbook to start a new one.

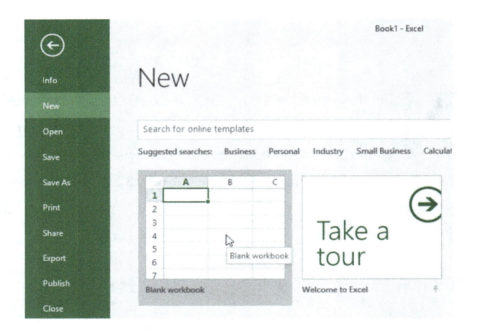

- From an Existing Workbook:
    - o   If you already have a workbook open, you can create a new one by clicking File > New > Blank Workbook from the File menu.

Step 3: Working in the New Workbook

- A new workbook will open with a single worksheet by default. You'll notice that Excel automatically gives the first sheet the name Sheet1. You can rename this sheet if desired (we'll discuss this in more detail later).

## Saving Your Work (Save vs. Save As)

Saving your work is crucial to prevent losing data. Excel offers two options when saving a workbook: Save and Save As. Let's take a look at each.

Step 1: Save

- To save your work, click File in the Ribbon, and then click Save. If you haven't saved the workbook before, Excel will prompt you to choose a location on your computer and give the file a name.
    - Shortcut for Save: You can also press Ctrl + S on your keyboard to quickly save your document.

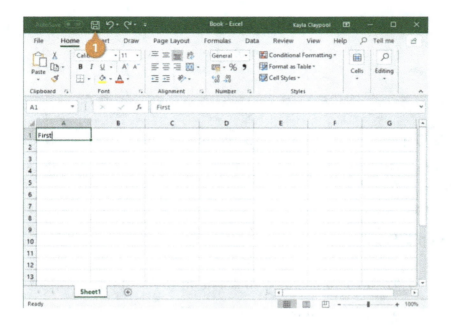

Step 2: Save As

- Save As is used when you want to create a copy of the
  workbook or save it in a different location or format. For
  example, if you want to save the workbook with a new name
  or to a different folder:
  - Click File > Save As.
  - Choose where you'd like to save the file (e.g., This PC,
    OneDrive).
  - Enter a new file name and click Save.

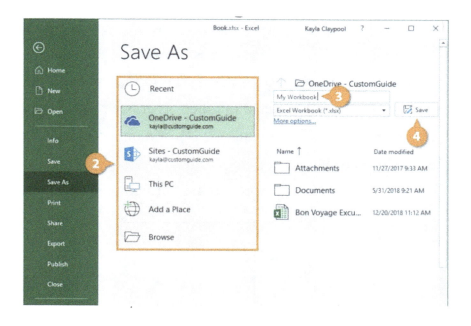

Why Use Save As?

- o You might want to create a backup of your work or save your document in a different format, such as PDF.
- o Save As allows you to change the location or format, while Save keeps the file in its original place.

## File Formats (XLSX, CSV, PDF, etc.)

When saving your workbook, Excel gives you several options for file formats. The most common formats include:

- XLSX (Excel Workbook): This is the default format for Excel files and is compatible with most versions of Excel.

- CSV (Comma Separated Values): This format is used for data that needs to be opened in other programs or shared with others. It's useful for data that is just numbers or text, with no formatting.

- PDF: A PDF file is a non-editable format, ideal for sharing finalized documents.

Step 3: Saving in Different Formats

- If you want to save your workbook as a PDF or CSV, you can click File > Save As, and then select the format from the "Save as type" dropdown.
    - PDF: Great for sharing a version that cannot be edited.
    - CSV: Ideal for spreadsheets with only data, no formatting.

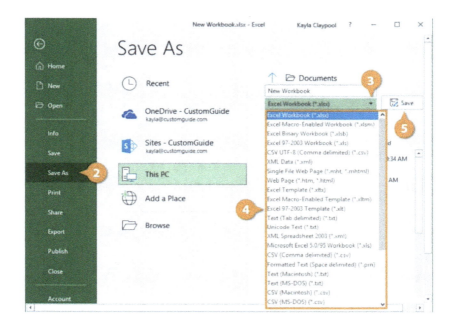

Summary

In this section, we:

- Started a new workbook, either from the Excel start screen or from an existing file.
- Learned how to save your work using both Save and Save As, including understanding different file formats such as XLSX, CSV, and PDF.
- Explored how to create, manage, and navigate through multiple worksheets within a workbook.

# Chapter 13. Working with Data in Excel

In this section, we will cover the essential techniques for working with data in Excel. Whether you're entering simple text, numbers, or using formulas to automate calculations, understanding how to efficiently work with data is the foundation of any good spreadsheet.

Let's dive into the steps for entering and editing data, using Autofill for faster input, and managing data with copy, cut, and paste operations.

## Entering and Editing Data

Step 1: Entering Data into a Cell

- Excel organizes data into cells, which are the individual boxes on a spreadsheet. Each cell is identified by its address — a combination of the column letter and row number (e.g., A1, B3).

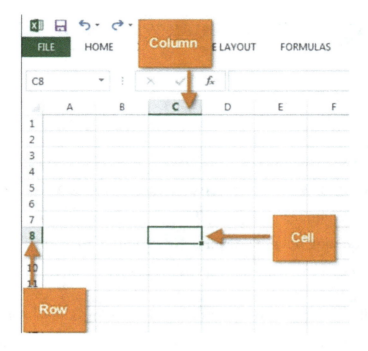

Cell, Row and Column in Excel Worksheet

To enter data:

1. Click on the cell where you want to enter the data.
2. Start typing the text, number, or formula you want to input.
3. Press Enter to move to the cell below, or use Tab to move to the next cell on the right.

Tip: If you want to keep editing the same cell, just press F2 to enter Edit Mode instead of typing directly.

Step 2: Editing Data in a Cell

- To edit data already entered into a cell:
    1. Double-click the cell, and the data will become editable.
    2. You can now change the data, and press Enter when finished, or click on another cell to apply the changes.

Step 3: Using the Formula Bar

- If the cell contains long text or a formula, you can edit it more easily by using the Formula Bar, located at the top of the Excel window.
    o Click into the Formula Bar, make your changes, and press Enter when done.

## Using Autofill and Quick Entry Techniques

Step 1: Using Autofill for Faster Data Entry

- Autofill is a powerful tool in Excel that lets you quickly fill in a series of data. For example, you can use it to extend a sequence of numbers, dates, or even copy formulas to other cells.

How to Use Autofill:

1. Enter data into a cell (e.g., "1" or a date like "January 1").
2. Hover your cursor over the small square at the bottom-right corner of the cell — this is called the fill handle.
3. When the cursor changes to a small black cross, click and drag the fill handle down (or across) to fill the cells with the series.
4. Release the mouse when you've selected the range of cells to fill.

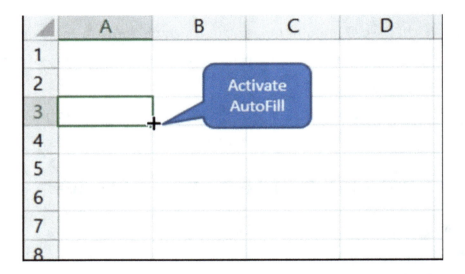

Tip: Excel will automatically recognize patterns (such as months, days, or numbers) and extend them. You can even create custom lists for autofilling.

Step 2: Quick Entry of Repeated Data

- For entering the same data in multiple cells, you can simply:
    1. Type the data into a cell.
    2. Select the cell and drag the fill handle to the other cells where you want the same data to appear.

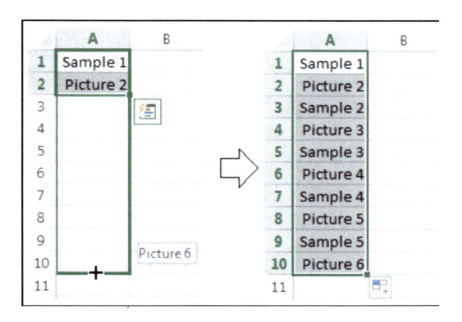

## Copying, Cutting, and Pasting Data

Step 1: Copying Data

- Copying allows you to duplicate data from one cell to another without altering the original data.

How to Copy Data:

1. Select the cell(s) that you want to copy.
2. Right-click and select Copy, or press Ctrl + C on your keyboard.
3. Select the destination cell(s) where you want to paste the copied data.
4. Right-click and select Paste, or press Ctrl + V on your keyboard.

Step 2: Cutting Data

- Cutting allows you to move data from one cell to another. This will remove the data from the original location.

How to Cut Data:

1. Select the cell(s) that you want to move.
2. Right-click and select Cut, or press Ctrl + X on your keyboard.
3. Select the destination cell(s) where you want the data moved.
4. Right-click and select Paste, or press Ctrl + V to paste the cut data.

Step 3: Paste Special

- If you want more control over how data is pasted (e.g., just values, formulas, or formatting), use the Paste Special options:

    1. After copying or cutting your data, right-click on the destination cell.
    2. Select Paste Special from the context menu and choose one of the available options (e.g., Values, Values and Number Formats, etc.).

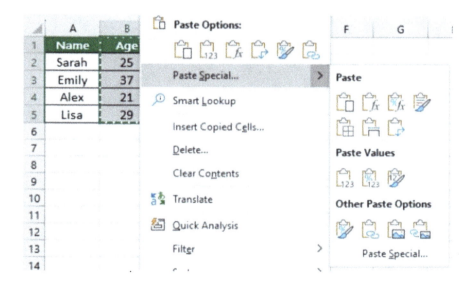

Summary

In this section, we've covered how to:

- Enter and edit data in Excel, including the use of the Formula Bar for longer or more complex data.
- Use Autofill to quickly fill in a series of numbers, dates, or text across cells.
- Manage data with Copy, Cut, and Paste, and learn about the Paste Special feature for advanced pasting options.

# Chapter 14. Formatting Your Spreadsheet

I n this section, we will explore how to format your spreadsheet to make it visually appealing and easy to read. Excel offers many options to adjust the appearance of your rows, columns, and cells. Proper formatting can improve the clarity of your data and make your spreadsheets more professional.

Let's walk through the steps for adjusting row height and column width, formatting cells, and applying cell styles for consistency.

## Adjusting Row Height and Column Width

Step 1: Adjusting Row Height

- Row height controls the vertical size of a row. By default, rows are set to a standard height, but you can change it to fit your data.

To Adjust Row Height:

1. Select the row(s) you want to resize by clicking on the row number on the left-hand side.
2. Hover your cursor over the bottom border of the selected row. The cursor will change to a double arrow.
3. Click and drag the border up or down to increase or decrease the row height.
4. Release the mouse when you have the desired height.

Tip: For automatic adjustment based on the largest content in the row, double-click on the row's bottom border.

Step 2: Adjusting Column Width

- Column width determines how wide a column is and impacts how much text or numbers fit in each cell. Adjusting column width is especially useful for making sure that all your data fits neatly in the spreadsheet.

To Adjust Column Width:

1. Select the column(s) you want to resize by clicking on the column letter at the top of the spreadsheet.
2. Hover your cursor over the right border of the selected column. The cursor will change to a double arrow.

3. Click and drag the border left or right to adjust the column width.
4. Release the mouse when you have the desired width.

Tip: To auto-fit the column width based on the longest content, double-click the right border of the column header.

## Formatting Cells: Text Alignment, Font, and Colors

Step 1: Text Alignment

- Excel allows you to adjust how text is aligned within cells — you can align text to the left, center, or right, both horizontally and vertically.

**To Change Text Alignment:**

1. Select the cell(s) you want to format.
2. On the Home tab in the Ribbon, look for the Alignment group.
3. Click on the alignment buttons:
    - Align Left: Aligns text to the left of the cell.
    - Center: Centers the text in the cell.
    - Align Right: Aligns text to the right of the cell.
    - Top Align, Middle Align, or Bottom Align to adjust vertical positioning.

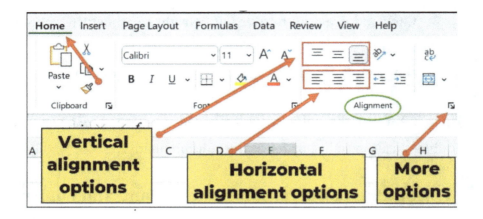

Step 2: Changing the Font

- You can customize the font style, size, and color to make your data stand out and improve readability.

**To Change the Font:**

1. Select the cell(s) whose font you want to change.
2. On the Home tab, in the Font group, you'll see options for Font Style, Font Size, and Font Color.
3. Choose a font style (e.g., Arial, Calibri) from the dropdown list.

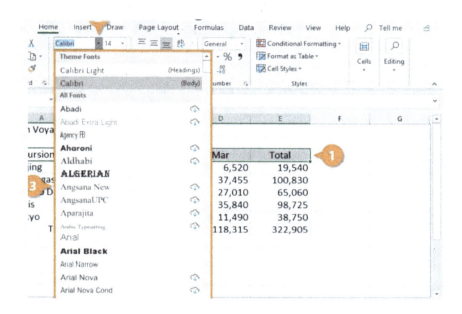

4.  Select a font size that suits your document.

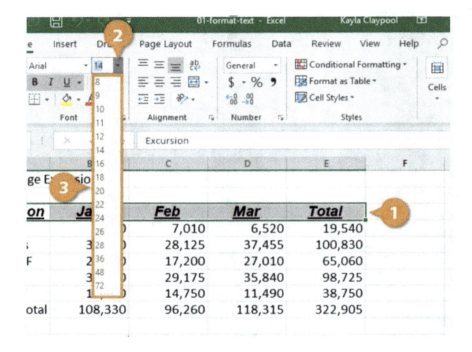

5. To change the font color, click on the Font Color button and pick a color from the color palette.

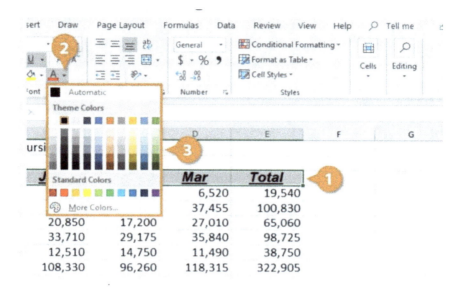

Step 3: Adding Background Colors

- You can add a background color to cells to help categorize data or draw attention to certain cells.

**To Add a Background Color:**

1. Select the cell(s) you want to format.
2. On the Home tab, in the Font group, click the Fill Color button (paint bucket icon).
3. Choose a color from the color palette. The background of the selected cells will change to the chosen color.

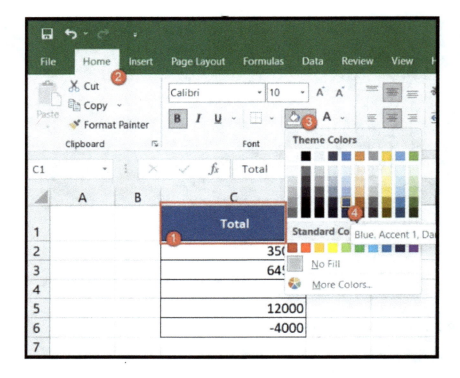

## Using Cell Styles for Consistency

Excel provides pre-defined cell styles to help you format your data consistently without having to manually adjust the font, color, and alignment every time.

Step 1: Applying a Cell Style

1. Select the cell(s) you want to format.
2. On the Home tab, in the Styles group, click on Cell Styles.

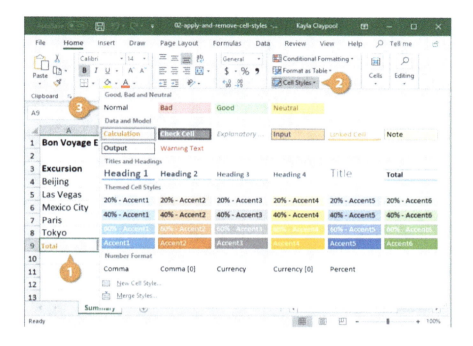

3. Choose a style from the available options (e.g., Good, Bad, Neutral, or Heading 1, etc.).

4. The selected style will automatically apply the formatting to the cells.

Tip: Using consistent cell styles throughout your spreadsheet can improve the overall design and make it look more polished.

Summary

In this section, we covered the essentials of formatting your spreadsheet:

- Adjusting row height and column width to ensure that all your data fits properly.
- Formatting cells by changing text alignment, font styles, sizes, and colors for better readability.
- Using cell styles to quickly and consistently format your data for a polished look.

# Chapter 15. Performing Basic Calculations

I n this section, we will delve into performing basic calculations in Excel. Calculations are one of the primary reasons to use Excel, and this section will teach you the essential skills you need to handle numbers efficiently. You'll learn how to use formulas and functions to perform tasks like summing numbers, finding averages, and more.

We'll also explore the difference between relative and absolute cell references, which is crucial for creating formulas that can be copied and reused.

## Understanding Formulas and Functions

Formulas and functions are at the heart of Excel's calculation capabilities. Here's a breakdown:

- Formulas: A formula is a mathematical expression that performs a calculation. It always starts with an equal sign =

and can include numbers, operators (like +, -, *, /), and cell references.

- Functions: Functions are pre-built formulas in Excel that simplify common calculations. Instead of writing out a long formula, you can use a function like SUM(), AVERAGE(), MIN(), etc.

Example of a Formula:

= A1 + B1

This formula adds the values in cells A1 and B1.

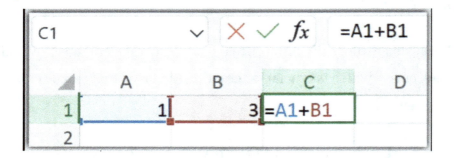

Example of a Function:

= SUM(A1:A5)

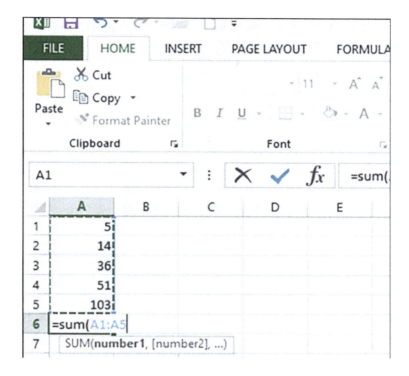

This function sums the values in cells A1 through A5.

## Using SUM, AVERAGE, MIN, MAX

Now that we understand formulas and functions, let's look at some of the most commonly used functions in Excel.

Step 1: Using the SUM Function The SUM() function adds up all the numbers in a range of cells.

To use the SUM function:

1. Click on the cell where you want the result to appear.
2. Type =SUM( to begin the function.
3. Select the range of cells you want to sum. For example, if you want to sum cells from A1 to A5, select those cells.
4. Press Enter to complete the formula.

Example:

=SUM(A1:A5)

This will sum all values in cells A1 through A5.

Step 2: Using the AVERAGE Function The AVERAGE() function calculates the mean of a set of numbers.

To use the AVERAGE function:

1. Click on the cell where you want the result to appear.
2. Type =AVERAGE( to begin the function.
3. Select the range of cells you want to average. For example, if you want to find the average of cells A1 to A5, select those cells.
4. Press Enter.

Example:

=AVERAGE(A1:A5)

This will return the average value of the cells from A1 to A5.

Step 3: Using the MIN and MAX Functions The MIN() function returns the smallest number in a range, and the MAX() function returns the largest number.

To use the MIN or MAX function:

1. Click on the cell where you want the result to appear.
2. Type =MIN( or =MAX( to begin the function.
3. Select the range of cells you want to analyze.
4. Press Enter.

Examples:

=MIN(A1:A5)

This will return the smallest value from cells A1 to A5.

=MAX(A1:A5)

This will return the largest value from cells A1 to A5.

# Relative vs. Absolute Cell References

When you create formulas in Excel, understanding the difference between relative and absolute cell references is crucial for making your formulas dynamic and flexible.

**Relative Cell References:**

- By default, Excel uses relative cell references, which change when you copy or move a formula to another cell. This is useful when you want the formula to adjust automatically based on the new location.

For example, if you have a formula in cell B1:

= A1 + B1

If you copy this formula from cell B1 to B2, Excel will automatically adjust the cell references:

= A2 + B2

Another example of how relative cell references work in Excel:

If we have 2 numbers in row A—A1 and A2. If we apply the formular =A1+A2, it would yield the result 200 in cell A3

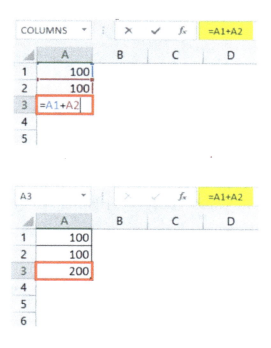

If we have a similar scenario in the column B that we need to sum along the same row to get B3.

We can decide to physically write the formula =B1+B2 to get the result for B3

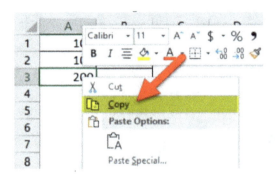

Alternatively, we could copy (by right-clicking) and paste the formula from cell A3 into B3.

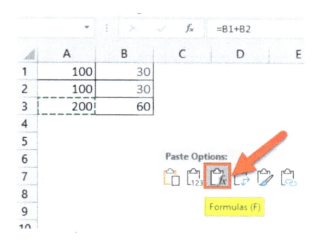

We will also achieve the same result by dragging the result from cell A3 to cell B3. It will copy the formula from column A and reference it relative to the new column B. You can see that the formula bar will give =B1+B2 even though what we copied or dragged was =A1+A2. Although we copied the answer 200 from A3, B3 still had its own answer relative to column B. That is a relative cell reference.

Remember, if we copy the formula that has a relative cell reference to another column that is in the same row, the column reference will be changed accordingly. For example:

| B1 ▾ ⋮ | =A1*10 |
| --- | --- |

| | A | B |
| --- | --- | --- |
| 1 | 1 | 10 |
| 2 | 2 | 20 |
| 3 | 3 | 30 |

| C1 ▾ ⋮ | =B1*10 |
| --- | --- |

| | A | B | C |
| --- | --- | --- | --- |
| 1 | 1 | 10 | 100 |
| 2 | 2 | 20 | 200 |
| 3 | 3 | 30 | 300 |

In column A we have items for sale. Column B contains the price of the items in USD. Column C is meant for the price of the same items in EUR. It has not been entered. If the conversion rate of USD to EUR is 0.93, in column C, row 2, we enter the formula =B2*0.93. Press enter and you will have the price of Apples in Euros.

| C2 ▾ ⋮ | =B2*0.93 |
| --- | --- |

| | A | B | C |
| --- | --- | --- | --- |
| 1 | Item | Price, USD | Price, EUR |
| 2 | Apples | $5.00 | €4.65 |
| 3 | Avocados | $4.50 | |
| 4 | Bananas | $3.90 | |
| 5 | Grapes | $9.90 | |
| 6 | Lemons | $4.70 | |
| 7 | Pears | $2.40 | |
| 8 | Watermelon | $2.50 | |

To get the Euro prices of the remaining items, you don't need to enter formula for each of them. If you drag the first cell down the column. (hover your mouse over the fill handle. (a small square in the bottom-right corner of the cell selected) and autofill)

| | A | B | C |
|---|---|---|---|
| 1 | Item | Price, USD | Price, EUR |
| 2 | Apples | $5.00 | €4.65 |
| 3 | Avocados | $4.50 | |
| 4 | Bananas | $3.90 | |
| 5 | Grapes | $9.90 | |
| 6 | Lemons | $4.70 | |
| 7 | Pears | $2.40 | |
| 8 | Watermelon | $2.50 | |

Hold and drag over the cells to which you want to copy the formula.

That is all you have to do! The formula is copied to all the other cells and the relative reference is adjusted accurately for each individual cell. If you select C4, for example, you will discover that the cell reference has been adjusted relative to row 4, which is different from the formula copied.

| C4 | ▼ ⋮ | =B4*0.93 |

| | A | B | C |
|---|---|---|---|
| 1 | Item | Price, USD | Price, EUR |
| 2 | Apples | $5.00 | €4.65 |
| 3 | Avocados | $4.50 | €4.19 |
| 4 | Bananas | $3.90 | €3.63 |
| 5 | Grapes | $9.90 | €9.21 |
| 6 | Lemons | $4.70 | €4.37 |
| 7 | Pears | $2.40 | €2.23 |
| 8 | Watermelon | $2.50 | €2.33 |

**Absolute Cell References:**

- If you want to lock a specific cell in a formula (so that it doesn't change when you copy the formula), you use absolute cell references by adding a dollar sign $ before the row and column.

$A$1

Locks column     Locks row

For example:

= $A$1 + B1

This formula always refers to A1 even if it is copied to another cell.

To better understand absolute reference, consider the image illustration below that shows how absolute reference and relative reference affected the results obtained.

| Absolute reference | | | | Relative reference | | |
|---|---|---|---|---|---|---|
| B3 ▼ : | =$A$1+5 | | | B3 ▼ : | =A1+5 | |

Absolute reference:

| | A | B |
|---|---|---|
| 1 | 10 | 15 |
| 2 | 9 | 15 |
| 3 | 8 | 15 |
| 4 | 7 | 15 |
| 5 | 6 | 15 |
| 6 | 5 | 15 |

Relative reference:

| | A | B |
|---|---|---|
| 1 | 10 | 15 |
| 2 | 9 | 14 |
| 3 | 8 | 13 |
| 4 | 7 | 12 |
| 5 | 6 | 11 |
| 6 | 5 | 10 |

To toggle between relative and absolute references:

- Press F4 after selecting a cell reference in a formula. This will toggle through the different reference types:
    - A1: Relative reference
    - $A$1: Absolute reference
    - A$1: Mixed reference (fixed row)

167

      ○   $A1: Mixed reference (fixed column)

## Summary

In this section, we've learned how to:

- Use basic functions like SUM(), AVERAGE(), MIN(), and MAX() to perform simple calculations.
- Understand the difference between relative and absolute cell references to create flexible formulas.
- Apply these functions and formulas in your spreadsheet to analyze and work with data more effectively.

# Chapter 16. Visualizing Data with Charts

C harts are a powerful tool in Excel that allow you to turn raw data into visual representations, making it easier to analyze, compare, and present information. Whether you're working with sales data, survey results, or any other numerical dataset, charts help you communicate insights clearly and effectively.

In this section, we'll explore how to create and customize bar charts, line charts, and pie charts. We'll also go over how to add data labels, legends, and how to personalize your charts to suit your needs.

## Creating Bar, Line, and Pie Charts

There are different types of charts, and each serves a unique purpose. Here, we will focus on three of the most common charts used in Excel: Bar charts, Line charts, and Pie charts.

Step 1: Creating a Bar Chart

A bar chart is useful when you want to compare quantities across different categories.

1. First, select the data you want to visualize. Make sure you include both the labels and the values (e.g., category names and their corresponding data).

| | A | B | C | D | E |
|---|---|---|---|---|---|
| 1 | Month | Bears | Dolphins | Whales | |
| 2 | Jan | 8 | 150 | 80 | |
| 3 | Feb | 54 | 77 | 54 | |
| 4 | Mar | 93 | 32 | 100 | |
| 5 | Apr | 116 | 11 | 76 | |
| 6 | May | 137 | 6 | 93 | |
| 7 | Jun | 184 | 1 | 72 | |
| 8 | | | | | |

2. Go to the Insert tab in the Ribbon.
3. In the Charts section, click on the Bar Chart icon. You'll see several options like Clustered Bar, Stacked Bar, etc. Choose the chart type that best fits your needs (we'll use Clustered Bar for this example).

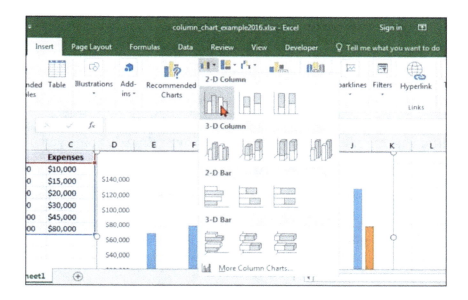

4. Your chart will appear in the spreadsheet, displaying your data in a bar format.

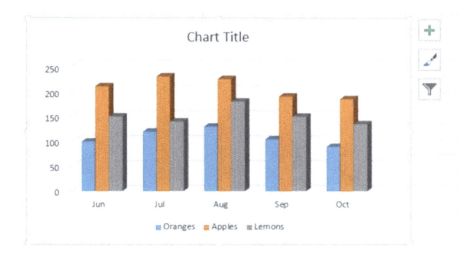

Example: If you have sales data by month, the months will be displayed on the x-axis, and the sales values on the y-axis as bars.

Step 2: Creating a Line Chart

A line chart is ideal for showing trends over time. It helps visualize how values change across a continuous range.

1. Select your data, just like you did for the bar chart.
2. Go to the Insert tab, and in the Charts section, click on the Line Chart icon.

3. Click Line with Markers.

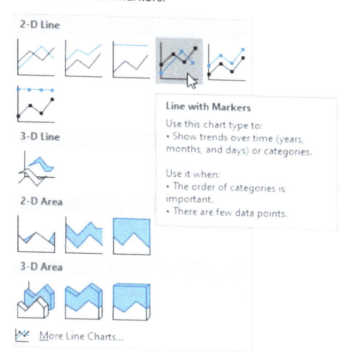

3. Choose the desired line chart style (e.g., Line with Markers).

4. The chart will automatically generate, showing the data points connected by a line.

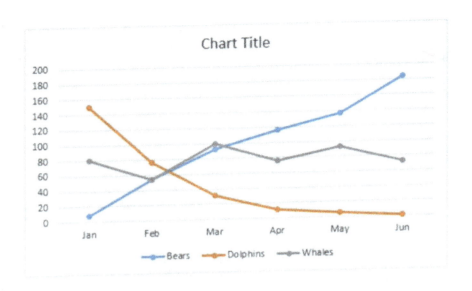

## Step 3: Creating a Pie Chart

A pie chart is best for showing how different parts contribute to a whole. It's ideal when you want to display proportions.

1. Select the data you want to visualize, such as categories and their percentages or values.

2. Go to the Insert tab, and click on the Pie Chart icon in the Charts section.

3. Choose a pie chart style (e.g., 2-D Pie).

4. The pie chart will be generated, with each segment representing a proportion of the whole.

# Customizing Chart Styles and Layouts

Once your chart is created, you can further customize it to make it visually appealing and easy to understand. Here are some common customization options:

Step 1: Changing the Chart Style

1. Click on the chart you just created to select it.
2. The Chart Tools will appear in the Ribbon, offering Design and Format tabs.
3. Under the Design tab, look for the Chart Styles group. Here, you can choose from different predefined styles to change the look of your chart (color scheme, background, etc.).
4. Select a style that best suits your needs.

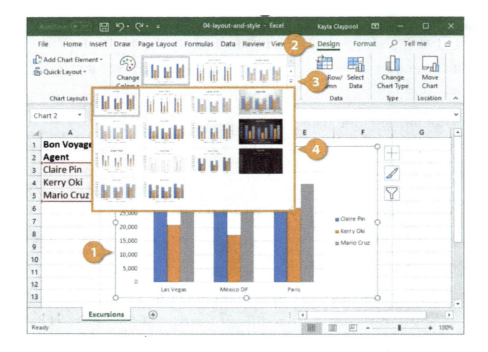

Step 2: Changing the Layout

1.  In the Design tab, also look for the Chart Layouts section.
2.  Choose from a variety of layouts that position elements like titles, axis labels, and legends in different ways.

## Adding Data Labels and Legends

Data labels and legends help provide clarity to your chart, making it easier for others to interpret.

Step 1: Adding Data Labels

Data labels show the actual values of the data points on the chart.

1. Click on the chart to select it.
2. In the Chart Tools section of the Ribbon, go to the Design tab.
3. Click Add Chart Element, and from the dropdown, choose Data Labels.
4. Select where you want the data labels to appear (e.g., Center, Outside End, etc.).

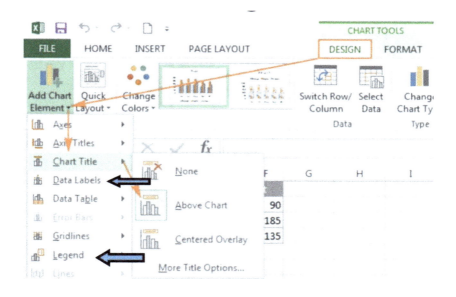

Alternatively, after selecting the chart, click the click the *Chart Elements* button in the upper-right corner of the chart, and select the **data labels** option.

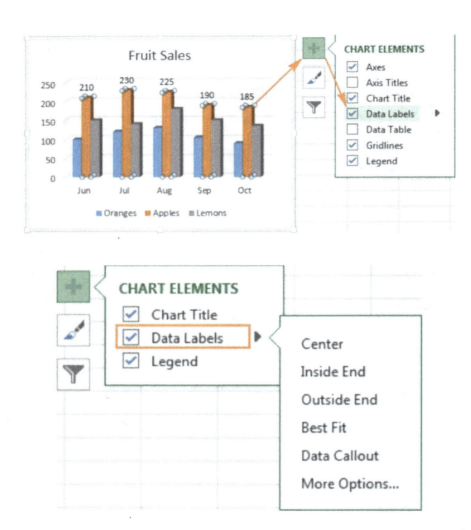

If you want to change what is written on the data labels in your chart, select *Chart Elements* button > *Data Labels* > *More options*. Select the **Label Options** tab and select the options you want the label to contain.

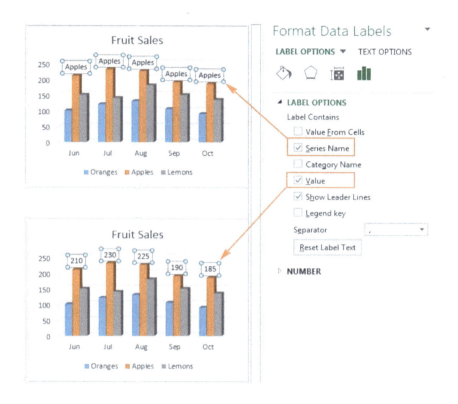

Step 2: Adding Legends

Legends are used to explain what each color or pattern in the chart represents. Excel usually adds a legend automatically, but you can adjust its position if needed.

1. Select the chart.
2. In the Design tab, click Add Chart Element and choose Legend.

3. You can choose from Right, Top, Left, or Bottom placement for the legend, depending on your preference.

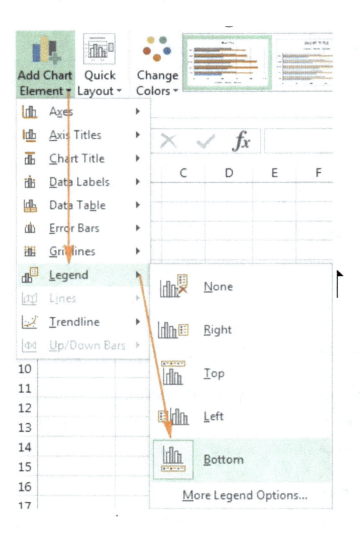

Another way to move the legend is to double-click on it in the chart, and then choose the desired legend position on the *Format Legend* pane under *Legend Options*.

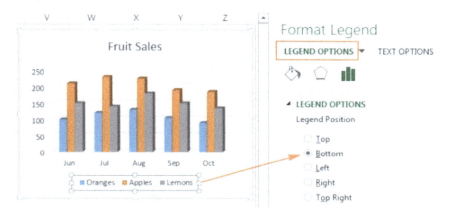

Summary

In this section, we learned how to:

- Create bar, line, and pie charts to visualize data in Excel.
- Customize the style and layout of charts to fit your needs.
- Add data labels and legends to provide more information to your viewers.

# Chapter 17. Working with Tables

I n Excel, tables are a powerful tool that allow you to organize, analyze, and present data in a structured and efficient way. When you convert a range of data into a table, Excel provides various built-in features such as sorting, filtering, and formatting options to make working with large datasets easier.

In this section, we'll go over how to convert data into a table, sort and filter data, and apply formatting to tables for better clarity and presentation.

## Converting Data into a Table

Before you can start taking advantage of all the table features in Excel, you need to convert your range of data into a table. This will unlock additional functionality, such as automatic column headers, sorting, and filtering options.

Step 1: Selecting Your Data

1. First, highlight the data you want to convert into a table. This should include both the column headings (like "Name", "Sales", "Date") and the actual data rows.

Step 2: Converting the Data into a Table

2. With the data selected, go to the Insert tab in the Ribbon.
3. In the Tables section, click on Table.
4. Excel will show a dialog box. Ensure the checkbox labeled My table has headers is checked (this tells Excel that the first row contains your column headings).
5. Click OK, and your data will now be converted into a table format.

Now, your data is organized in a structured format that is easier to manage and analyze.

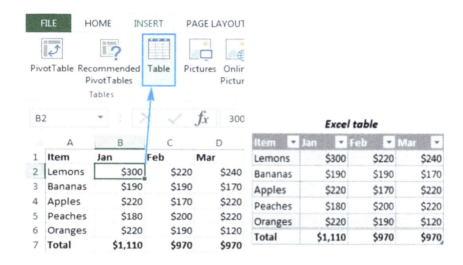

# Sorting and Filtering Data

Once your data is in a table, you can use Excel's built-in sorting and filtering features to quickly rearrange or focus on specific parts of your data.

Step 1: Sorting Data

Sorting allows you to organize your data in ascending or descending order based on one or more columns.

1. Click the dropdown arrow next to the column header you want to sort by (for example, "Sales" or "Date").
2. You'll see two options:

- Sort A to Z: Sorts the data in ascending order (smallest to largest, alphabetically).

- Sort Z to A: Sorts the data in descending order (largest to smallest, reverse alphabetical).

3. Click the appropriate sorting option, and your data will rearrange accordingly.

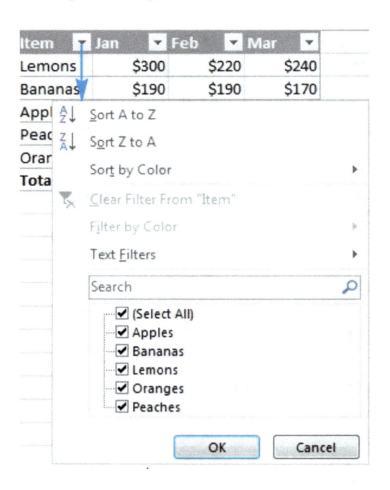

Step 2: Filtering Data

Filtering enables you to view only the rows that meet certain criteria, hiding the rest. This is useful when working with large datasets.

1. Click the dropdown arrow next to the column header you want to filter (for example, "Category" or "Date").
2. Check the box next to the values you want to display. You can select multiple items or use the search box to quickly find specific values.
3. Click OK, and Excel will only show the rows that match the filter criteria. The rest will be hidden.
4. To remove the filter, click the dropdown arrow again and select Clear Filter from [Column Name].

## Adding Totals and Formatting Tables

Adding totals and applying formatting can help make your table easier to read and more visually appealing.

Step 1: Adding Totals to a Table

Excel makes it easy to calculate totals, averages, and other summary statistics for the data in your table.

1. Click anywhere inside the table.

2. Go to the Table Design tab in the Ribbon.

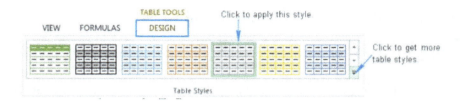

3. In the Table Style Options section, check the box labeled Total Row.

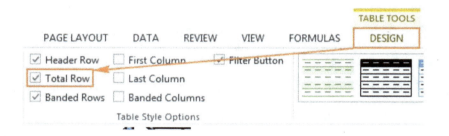

4. A row will appear at the bottom of your table. This row can automatically calculate totals for numerical columns, as well as averages, counts, and other calculations.

5. Click any cell in the Total Row, and from the dropdown menu, select the calculation you want to perform (e.g., Sum, Average, Count).

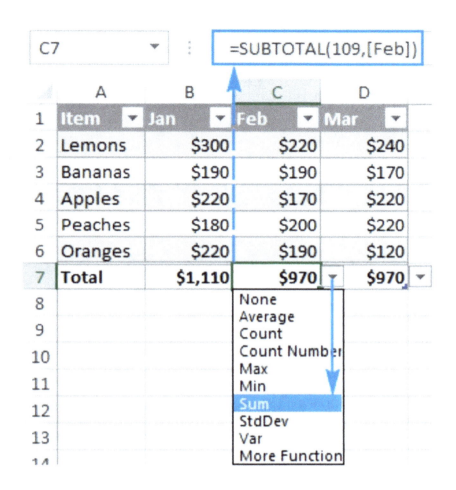

| | A | B | C | D |
|---|---|---|---|---|
| 1 | Item ▼ | Jan ▼ | Feb ▼ | Mar ▼ |
| 2 | Lemons | $300 | $220 | $240 |
| 3 | Bananas | $190 | $190 | $170 |
| 4 | Apples | $220 | $170 | $220 |
| 5 | Peaches | $180 | $200 | $220 |
| 6 | Oranges | $220 | $190 | $120 |
| 7 | Total | $1,110 | $970 ▼ | $970 ▼ |

C7    =SUBTOTAL(109,[Feb])

None
Average
Count
Count Number
Max
Min
Sum
StdDev
Var
More Function

## Step 2: Formatting Tables

Excel allows you to apply different styles and formatting options to your table, making it look professional and easier to read.

1. Click anywhere inside the table.

2. Go to the Table Design tab.

3. In the Table Styles section, choose a style from the options available. There are various preset styles that adjust color, borders, and shading for alternate rows to improve readability.

4. If you want to further customize the formatting, you can adjust the font size, color, or add borders through the Home tab on the Ribbon.

Summary

In this section, we learned how to:

- Convert a range of data into a table to access advanced features.
- Sort and filter data to organize and analyze it effectively.
- Add totals and apply formatting to improve the appearance and clarity of tables.

# Chapter 18. Collaboration and Sharing in Excel

E xcel provides powerful collaboration tools that make it easier to work on documents with others. Whether you're working in a team or need to share a report with someone, Excel's real-time collaboration features and integration with OneDrive and other cloud services help ensure smooth communication and efficient teamwork.

In this section, we'll walk through how to share workbooks, collaborate in real-time, and manage workbook versions. These skills are essential for working in today's interconnected digital environment.

## Sharing Workbooks via OneDrive

Sharing workbooks through OneDrive allows you to access your Excel file from anywhere and collaborate with others in real-time. To get started, you first need to save your workbook to OneDrive.

Step 1: Saving to OneDrive

1. Open your Excel workbook and go to the File tab.
2. Click on Save As.
3. Under Save As, select OneDrive – Personal (or your organization's OneDrive, if applicable).
4. Choose the folder where you want to save the file and click Save. Now your workbook is stored in the cloud and accessible from any device with an internet connection.

Step 2: Sharing the Workbook: note that your workbooks must be saved to OneDrive or SharePoint before you can share them.

1. With the workbook open, click the Share button. You will see several options for sharing your file.
2. You can either:
   o Invite people by entering their email addresses and selecting their permission level (Can Edit or Can View).
   o Get a sharing link: Generate a link to send to others. You can choose whether people with the link can edit or only view the file.

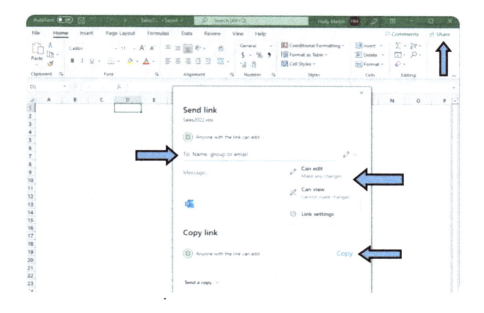

3. Click Apply and then share the link via email, message, or any communication platform you prefer.

Now, anyone you've shared the workbook with can access it from their devices.

## Co-Authoring in Real-Time

One of the best features of sharing a workbook via OneDrive is the ability to collaborate with others in real time. Co-authoring allows multiple people to work on the same Excel document at the same time, seeing each other's changes immediately.

Step 1: Collaborating in Real-Time

1. Once you have shared the workbook, ask the other person to open the workbook from their OneDrive or via the link you've shared.
2. As you both make edits, you will see each other's changes in real-time. Excel will highlight the changes in different colors to indicate who is editing what.
3. You will also see the names of the people working on the document at the top-right corner of the window.
4. If someone is editing a cell, it will show as locked for others until the person finishes editing.

Step 2: Communicating with Co-Authors

If you need to communicate with your co-author while working on the document, you can use the Comments feature:

1. Right-click on a cell and select New Comment. Alternately, you can click on the cell where you want to add the comment, click the review tab, and select the **New Comment** button

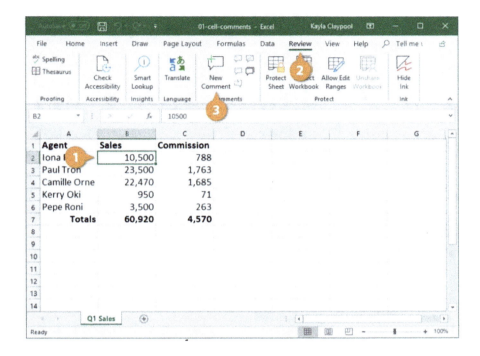

2. Type your message, and your co-author can reply directly to your comment.

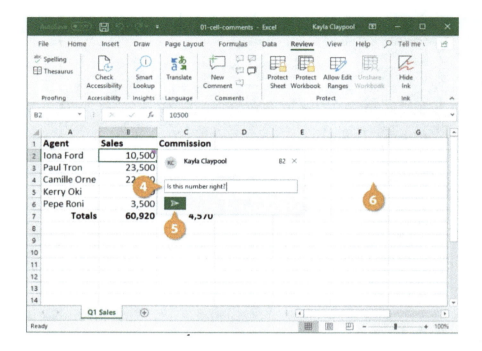

This makes it easy to clarify any questions or instructions while collaborating in real time.

## Managing Workbook Versions

Managing different versions of your workbook is important, especially when collaborating with others. Excel saves version history automatically, so you can view, restore, or compare previous versions of the document.

Step 1: Viewing Version History

1. Go to the File tab in Excel.

2. Click on Info in the left sidebar.

3. Under Version History, you will see a list of previously saved versions of your document.

4. Click on any version to open it. Excel will display a snapshot of that version, and you can choose to restore it by clicking Restore at the top.

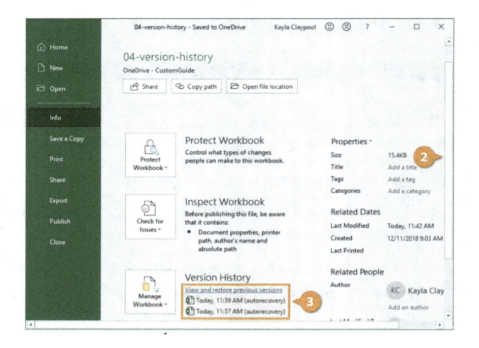

Step 2: Restoring a Previous Version

1.  If you've made changes that you want to undo or need to retrieve an earlier version, you can restore a previous version from the Version History menu.

2.  Select the version you want, and then click Restore. This will make that version the active one, but the current version will be saved as another version in case you need to go back to it.

Managing versions is helpful to track changes, recover work, and ensure that nothing gets lost.

## Summary

In this section, we explored how to:

- Share workbooks via OneDrive to make collaboration easy.
- Collaborate in real time with co-authors and communicate directly in the workbook.
- Manage workbook versions to keep track of changes and restore previous versions when necessary.

# 19. Printing and Exporting in Excel

When working with Excel, it's often necessary to print your spreadsheets or export them in a different format, such as a PDF or CSV. Whether you're preparing a report for a meeting or sharing a dataset with others, understanding how to set up your document for printing and exporting is crucial.

In this section, we will cover how to set up print areas, adjust page layouts, and export your workbook in different formats. This will help you present your data in a professional way and share it with others in various formats.

## Setting Up Print Areas

Before printing, you may want to define specific parts of your spreadsheet to print. This is especially useful when you don't need to print the entire worksheet but just a selected range of cells.

Step 1: Select the Print Area

1. Open your Excel workbook and select the range of cells you want to print. Click and drag your mouse to highlight the cells.

2. Once your desired range is selected, go to the Page Layout tab on the Ribbon.

3. In the Page Setup group, click on Print Area, then select Set Print Area. This will designate the selected cells as the print area.

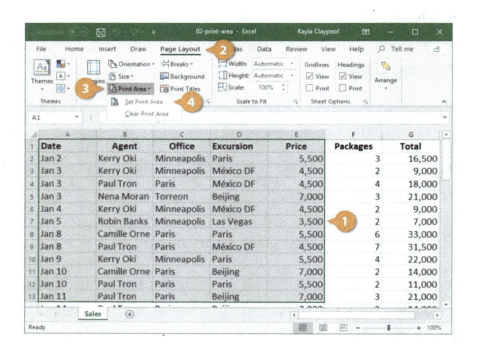

Step 2: Clear Print Areas (if needed)

1. If you want to remove the print area and select a new one, simply go to the Page Layout tab again.

2. In the Page Setup group, click Print Area, then select Clear Print Area. This will reset the print area for the entire worksheet.

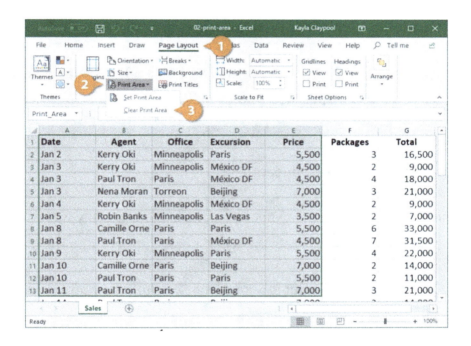

## Adjusting Page Layouts for Printing

Adjusting the page layout ensures that your spreadsheet fits neatly onto the printed page, making it look organized and professional.

Step 1: Set Page Orientation

1. Go to the Page Layout tab on the Ribbon.
2. In the Page Setup group, click on Orientation. You can choose between Portrait (vertical) or Landscape (horizontal) depending on the layout of your data.

Step 2: Adjust Paper Size

1. In the same Page Setup group, click on Size. You can select standard sizes like Letter (8.5 x 11 inches) or A4. If you need a custom paper size, you can click More Paper Sizes at the bottom.

Step 3: Scaling the Document to Fit

Sometimes, your data may not fit on one page, especially with large spreadsheets. You can scale the worksheet to fit better on the page:

1. In the Page Layout tab, go to the Scale to Fit group.
2. You can adjust the Width and Height to fit the page, or use the Scale option to set a percentage (for example, 75% of the original size).
3. To ensure everything fits on one page, you can check Fit to One Page for both width and height.

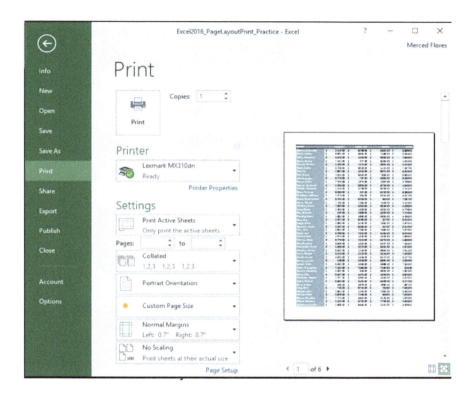

## Exporting as PDF or CSV

Excel allows you to export your workbook in various formats, such as PDF for sharing documents that are easy to read or CSV for datasets that can be used in other applications.

Step 1: Exporting as PDF

1. Click on the File tab in the Ribbon.
2. Select Export from the sidebar.
3. Choose Create PDF/XPS Document.

4. In the pop-up window, select the location where you want to save the file, and choose PDF as the format. You can also select options like Minimize Size (for email attachments) or Standard (for high-quality printing).
5. Click Publish to create the PDF file.

Step 2: Exporting as CSV

1. Again, click on the File tab.
2. Select Save As and choose the location where you want to save the file.
3. Under Save as type, select CSV (Comma delimited) (*.csv).
4. Choose a name for your file and click Save. Excel will warn you that some features (such as multiple sheets or formatting) will be lost in the CSV format. Click OK to confirm.

Summary

In this section, you learned how to:

- Set up print areas to select specific data to print.
- Adjust page layouts to ensure your document fits neatly on the page.

- Export your workbook as PDF or CSV for easy sharing and distribution.

# Chapter 20. Advanced Excel Skills for Beginners

As you become more comfortable with the basics of Excel, it's time to take your skills to the next level. In this section, we will dive into some advanced Excel features that will help you work more efficiently and powerfully with your data. We'll explore how to use Conditional Formatting, create PivotTables, and begin using Macros. These features are not only essential for organizing and analyzing data but also for automating tasks and creating professional reports.

## Using Conditional Formatting

Conditional Formatting allows you to apply different formatting styles (such as color or font changes) to cells based on the data they contain. This can help highlight trends, make data more readable, and emphasize key figures.

Step 1: Select the Range of Cells

1.  Open your Excel worksheet.

2. Select the range of cells where you want to apply conditional formatting. This could be a column, a row, or a block of data.

Step 2: Apply Conditional Formatting

1. Go to the Home tab on the Ribbon.
2. In the Styles group, click on Conditional Formatting.
3. A menu will appear with several options:
   - Highlight Cells Rules: This option allows you to highlight cells based on specific conditions (such as cells that are greater than or less than a certain value).
   - Top/Bottom Rules: Apply formatting to the top or bottom values in your selection.
   - Data Bars: This adds a colored bar inside the cells, visually representing the magnitude of the values.
   - Color Scales: Color gradients will represent the values in a range of colors.
   - Icon Sets: Adds icons (such as arrows or flags) based on the values in your cells.

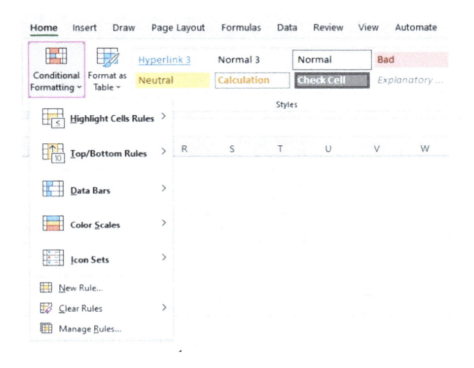

## Step 3: Customize Conditional Formatting

1. Once you've selected a formatting option (for example, Highlight Cells Rules > Less Than), a dialog box will appear.

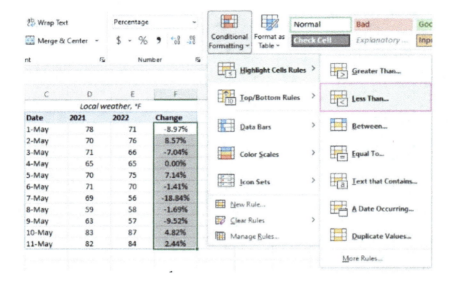

2. Enter the value that triggers the formatting and choose the formatting style (such as the font color or fill color).

3. Click OK to apply the formatting.

Step 4: Clear or Manage Conditional Formatting

1. To modify or remove your conditional formatting, go back to the Conditional Formatting button on the Ribbon.

2. Select Manage Rules to edit, delete, or modify existing rules.

3. To remove all conditional formatting, choose Clear Rules.

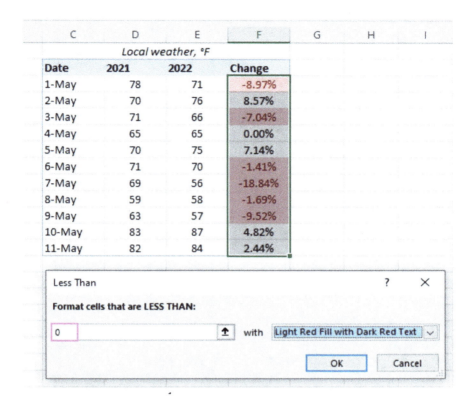

## Introduction to PivotTables

PivotTables are one of Excel's most powerful tools. They allow you to quickly summarize, analyze, and present your data in a dynamic way. With a PivotTable, you can rearrange (pivot) your data, create custom summaries, and generate insightful reports without having to manually reorganize your data.

The image illustration below shows data entries of sales figures of a retailer and examples of pivot tables formed.

| | A | B | C | D |
|---|---|---|---|---|
| 1 | **Product** | **Reseller** | **Month** | **Sales** |
| 2 | Cherries | John | Oct | $250 |
| 3 | Bananas | Mike | Nov | $200 |
| 4 | Apples | Pete | Oct | $180 |
| 5 | Oranges | Mike | Nov | $400 |
| 6 | Bananas | Sally | Oct | $250 |
| 7 | Apples | Mike | Oct | $120 |
| 8 | Cherries | Sally | Sep | $330 |
| 9 | Apples | Pete | Oct | $110 |
| 10 | Cherries | Mike | Sep | $250 |

**Pivot Table 1**

| Sales | Sep | Oct | Nov | Total |
|---|---|---|---|---|
| Apples | 250 | 590 | | 840 |
| John | | 180 | | 180 |
| Mike | | 120 | | 120 |
| Pete | | 290 | | 290 |
| Sally | 250 | | | 250 |
| Bananas | | 430 | 600 | 1030 |
| John | | | 400 | 400 |
| Mike | | | 200 | 200 |
| Pete | | 180 | | 180 |
| Sally | | 250 | | 250 |
| Cherries | 580 | 910 | | 1490 |
| John | | 250 | | 250 |
| Mike | 250 | 330 | | 580 |
| Pete | | 330 | | 330 |
| Sally | 330 | | | 330 |
| Oranges | | 120 | 720 | 840 |
| John | | | 120 | 120 |
| Mike | | | 400 | 400 |
| Pete | | 120 | | 120 |
| Sally | | | 200 | 200 |
| Total | 830 | 2050 | 1320 | 4200 |

**Pivot Table 2**

| Month | (All) |

| Sales | Product | | | | |
|---|---|---|---|---|---|
| Reseller | Apples | Bananas | Cherries | Oranges | Total |
| John | $180 | $400 | $250 | $120 | $950 |
| Mike | $120 | $200 | $580 | $400 | $1,300 |
| Pete | $290 | $180 | $330 | $120 | $920 |
| Sally | $250 | $250 | $330 | $200 | $1,030 |
| Total | $840 | $1,030 | $1,490 | $840 | $4,200 |

**Pivot Table 3**

| Product | (All) |

| Sales | Month | | | |
|---|---|---|---|---|
| Reseller | Sep | Oct | Nov | Total |
| John | | $430 | $520 | $950 |
| Mike | $250 | $450 | $600 | $1,300 |
| Pete | | $920 | | $920 |
| Sally | $580 | $250 | $200 | $1,030 |
| Total | $830 | $2,050 | $1,320 | $4,200 |

Step 1: Insert a PivotTable

1.  Open your workbook and select the data range you want to analyze.
2.  Go to the Insert tab on the Ribbon.
3.  Click on PivotTable in the Tables group.

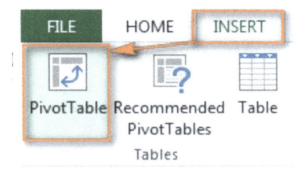

4.  In the Create PivotTable dialog box, ensure that the correct data range is selected. You can also choose to place the PivotTable in a new worksheet or in an existing one.
5.  Click OK.

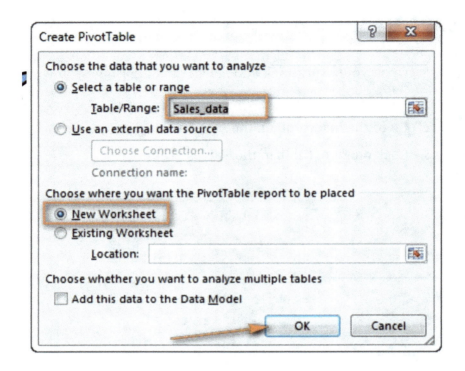

Step 2: Set Up Your PivotTable

1. On the right side of the screen, you will see the PivotTable Field List.

2. Drag the fields (column names from your dataset) into the appropriate areas:

    o   Rows: To group your data by rows.

    o   Columns: To group your data by columns.

    o   Values: To display data (such as sum, average, or count).

o Filters: To apply filters to your PivotTable (for example, filtering data by specific categories).

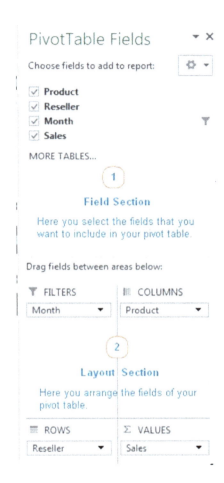

Step 3: Summarize and Analyze Your Data

1. Once you've placed fields in the appropriate areas, Excel will automatically summarize your data.

2. You can change how data is summarized (e.g., sum, average) by right-clicking on the value field and selecting Summarize Values By.

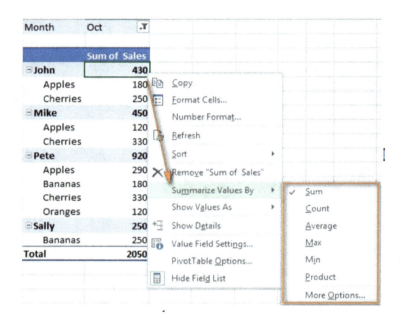

Step 4: Customize Your PivotTable

1. You can further customize the PivotTable layout by using the PivotTable Analyze and Design tabs on the Ribbon.

2. Use Design to apply different styles or change the layout of the PivotTable.

3. Use Analyze to group data, refresh the table, or add slicers for easier filtering.

# Creating Basic Macros

Macros in Excel are sequences of commands and actions that you can record and then play back to automate repetitive tasks. While advanced users may write their own macros using Visual Basic for Applications (VBA), beginners can get started by simply recording basic macros.

Step 1: Enable Macros

1. Before you can use macros, you need to ensure that macros are enabled:
    - Go to the File tab and click on Options.
    - In the Excel Options window, select Trust Center and click Trust Center Settings.
    - In the Macro Settings section, select Enable all macros and click OK.

Step 2: Record a Macro

1. Go to the View tab on the Ribbon.
2. In the Macros group, click Record Macro.
3. In the Record Macro dialog box:
    - Give your macro a name (e.g., "FormatData").
    - Assign a Shortcut Key if desired (e.g., Ctrl+Shift+F).

- o Choose where to store the macro: either in the current workbook or in a new workbook.

4. Click OK to start recording your macro.

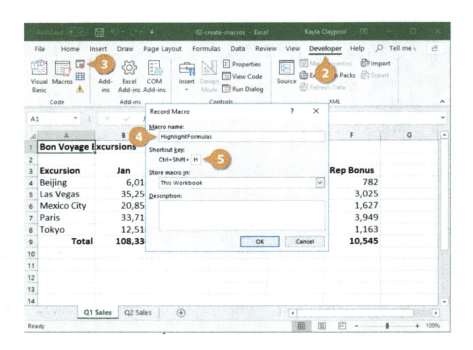

Step 3: Perform the Actions to Record

1. While recording, perform the actions you want the macro to execute. For example, you could select a range of cells, apply a specific font style, or change the color.

2. When you are done, go back to the View tab and click Stop Recording in the Macros group.

# Step 4: Run the Macro

1. To run your macro, go to the View tab and click Macros.

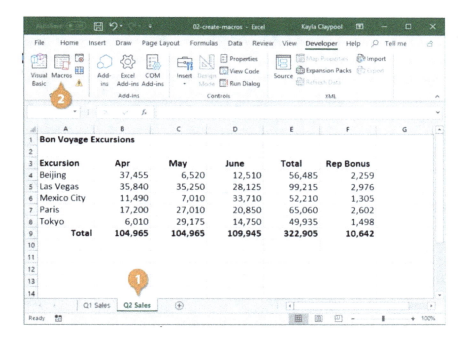

2. Select View Macros.

3. Choose your macro from the list and click Run.

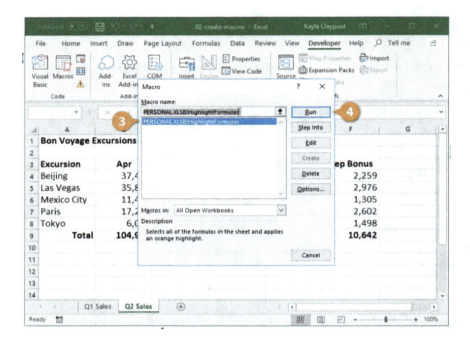

In this section, you learned about three advanced Excel skills:

- Conditional Formatting, which allows you to automatically format cells based on their values, helping you visualize trends and important data.

- PivotTables, a powerful tool for summarizing and analyzing data in a flexible and dynamic way.

- Macros, which allow you to automate repetitive tasks, saving you time and effort.

# Extras and Appendices

# Appendix A: Keyboard Shortcuts for Microsoft Word and Excel

**M**astering keyboard shortcuts can drastically improve your productivity and efficiency in Microsoft Word and Excel. Instead of relying on the mouse for every action, you can use simple key combinations to perform tasks more quickly. In this section, we will explore essential keyboard shortcuts for both Microsoft Word and Excel. We will also provide you with a handy chart to keep on hand for quick reference.

## Essential Shortcuts for Efficiency

### Microsoft Word Keyboard Shortcuts

1. Basic Navigation:
   - Ctrl + N: Open a new document.
   - Ctrl + O: Open an existing document.
   - Ctrl + S: Save the current document.
   - Ctrl + P: Open the Print menu.
   - Ctrl + F: Open the Find dialog to search within the document.

- Ctrl + H: Open the Replace dialog to search and replace text.

2. Text Editing:
   - Ctrl + C: Copy the selected text or object.
   - Ctrl + X: Cut the selected text or object.
   - Ctrl + V: Paste the copied or cut content.
   - Ctrl + Z: Undo the previous action.
   - Ctrl + Y: Redo the previous action.
   - Ctrl + A: Select all content in the document.

3. Formatting:
   - Ctrl + B: Bold the selected text.
   - Ctrl + I: Italicize the selected text.
   - Ctrl + U: Underline the selected text.
   - Ctrl + E: Center align the selected text.
   - Ctrl + L: Left align the selected text.
   - Ctrl + R: Right align the selected text.
   - Ctrl + J: Justify align the selected text.

4. Working with Paragraphs:
   - Ctrl + M: Increase paragraph indent.
   - Ctrl + Shift + M: Decrease paragraph indent.
   - Ctrl + T: Create a hanging indent.
   - Ctrl + Q: Remove paragraph formatting.

5. Special Features:
   - Ctrl + K: Insert or edit a hyperlink.

- Ctrl + L: Insert a left-aligned tab stop.
- Ctrl + Shift + C: Copy the formatting of the selected text.
- Ctrl + Shift + V: Paste the copied formatting onto new text.

## Microsoft Excel Keyboard Shortcuts

1. Basic Navigation:
   - Ctrl + N: Open a new workbook.
   - Ctrl + O: Open an existing workbook.
   - Ctrl + S: Save the current workbook.
   - Ctrl + P: Open the Print menu.
   - Ctrl + F: Open the Find dialog to search within the spreadsheet.
   - Ctrl + H: Open the Replace dialog to search and replace data.
2. Cell Selection and Editing:
   - Ctrl + C: Copy the selected cell(s).
   - Ctrl + X: Cut the selected cell(s).
   - Ctrl + V: Paste the copied or cut data.
   - Ctrl + Z: Undo the previous action.
   - Ctrl + Y: Redo the previous action.
   - Ctrl + A: Select all cells in the worksheet.
3. Working with Cells:

- o Ctrl + Shift + L: Turn on or off filters.
- o Ctrl + Shift + "+": Insert a new row or column.
- o Ctrl + "-": Delete the selected row or column.
- o Ctrl + D: Fill down (copy the content of the selected cell to the cells below).
- o Ctrl + R: Fill right (copy the content of the selected cell to the cells to the right).

4. Working with Data:
- o Alt + E, S, V: Paste Special options.
- o Ctrl + Shift + "$": Apply currency formatting.
- o Ctrl + Shift + "%": Apply percentage formatting.
- o Ctrl + Shift + "#": Apply date formatting.
- o Ctrl + T: Convert the selected data range into a table.
- o Ctrl + Shift + L: Apply or remove filters to columns.

5. Working with Formulas:
- o Alt + "=": AutoSum (sum the numbers in the selected cells).
- o Ctrl + Shift + Enter: Enter an array formula.
- o Ctrl + ~: Toggle between displaying cell values and formulas.
- o F2: Edit the active cell's content.
- o F4: Repeat the last action (such as formatting or inserting).

## Summary

By mastering these essential keyboard shortcuts, you will significantly improve your workflow and increase your efficiency in both Microsoft Word and Excel. Remember, the key to making the most of these shortcuts is consistent practice. Over time, using keyboard shortcuts will become second nature, allowing you to complete tasks faster and with less effort.

For easy reference, keep the shortcut chart nearby or print it out and place it next to your computer for quick access as you work.

# Appendix B: Troubleshooting Common Issues

In this appendix, we will address some of the most common issues you might encounter while working in Microsoft Word and Excel. Whether it's dealing with alignment problems in Word or resolving formula errors in Excel, we'll walk through practical solutions to ensure you can get back on track without frustration. We'll also include helpful screenshots to guide you through the troubleshooting process.

## Fixing Alignment Problems in Word

Alignment issues are a common challenge when working with text in Microsoft Word. Sometimes, text may not align as expected, especially when working with different fonts, indents, or when copying and pasting from other sources. Here's how you can fix these issues:

1. Text Alignment Issues

- Issue: Text may appear misaligned or uneven across the page.

  Solution:

  - Select the text that isn't aligned properly.
  - Navigate to the Home tab in the Ribbon.
  - In the Paragraph group, choose one of the following alignment options:
    - Align Left (Ctrl + L): Aligns the text to the left margin.
    - Center (Ctrl + E): Centers the text in the middle of the page.
    - Align Right (Ctrl + R): Aligns the text to the right margin.
    - Justify (Ctrl + J): Spreads the text so that it aligns with both the left and right margins, giving it a uniform edge.

  Tip: If you have a block of text and it's not aligning well, try adjusting the line spacing or margins for a better fit.

## 2. Indentation Issues

- Issue: Paragraphs are not indented properly or at all.

Solution:

  ○ Select the paragraph that has the indentation issue.
  ○ Go to the Home tab and look for the Paragraph group.
  ○ Use the Increase Indent (Ctrl + M) and Decrease Indent (Ctrl + Shift + M) buttons to adjust the indent.
  ○ For more control over indentation, click the small arrow in the bottom right corner of the Paragraph group to open the full Paragraph Settings window.
  ○ In the Indentation section, you can choose First Line or Hanging indent, as well as set precise measurements.

## Resolving Formula Errors in Excel

Formula errors in Excel can be frustrating, but they are easy to resolve once you know how to troubleshoot them. Below are some of the most common formula errors and their solutions.

1. #DIV/0! Error (Division by Zero)

- Issue: This error occurs when you attempt to divide a number by zero.

Solution:

- o Check the formula to ensure that the divisor is not zero or a blank cell.
- o Use the IFERROR function to prevent the error from appearing. Example: =IFERROR(A1/B1, "Error")
- o This formula will return "Error" instead of showing #DIV/0! if B1 is zero or blank.

## 2. #VALUE! Error (Wrong Data Type)

- Issue: This error occurs when a formula receives a value of the wrong data type.

Solution:

- o Review the data types in the cells involved in the formula. Ensure that all numeric values are indeed numbers and not text.
- o If the formula includes text values that need to be converted to numbers, use the VALUE function. Example: =VALUE(A1) will convert a text-based number into a numeric value.

3. #REF! Error (Invalid Cell Reference)

- Issue: This occurs when a formula refers to a cell that no longer exists or is incorrectly referenced.

  Solution:

  - Check the formula to make sure all cell references are valid. You might have deleted a row or column that was part of the formula.
  - If needed, replace the invalid cell reference with the correct one.

4. #N/A Error (Value Not Available)

- Issue: This error typically appears when a lookup function (such as VLOOKUP or HLOOKUP) cannot find a match.

  Solution:

  - Verify that the data you are looking up is present and formatted consistently across both the lookup table and the formula.
  - Use the IFERROR function to replace the error with a more user-friendly message. Example:

```
=IFERROR(VLOOKUP(A1, B1:B10, 1, FALSE), "Not
Found")
```

Summary

In this appendix, we've addressed some common issues you might face when working with Microsoft Word and Excel, including alignment problems and formula errors. By following the troubleshooting steps outlined above, you can easily resolve these issues and get back to work. Don't hesitate to refer to these tips whenever you run into problems in Word or Excel—solving these problems will help you work more efficiently and confidently.

# Appendix C: Glossary of Terms

In this appendix, we'll provide a glossary of common terms used in Microsoft Word and Excel, along with easy-to-understand definitions. These terms are essential to know as you use the applications, and having a clear understanding of them will help you navigate Word and Excel with greater ease and confidence.

## Common Terms in Microsoft Word

1. Ribbon

The Ribbon is the top section of the Word interface, where you'll find various tabs and tools to help you edit and format your document. Each tab (such as Home, Insert, and Layout) contains different options related to specific tasks.

2. Quick Access Toolbar

This is a small toolbar located at the top of the Word window. It provides quick access to commonly used tools like Save, Undo, and Redo. You can customize the Quick Access Toolbar to include any tool you use often.

## 3. Status Bar

The Status Bar is located at the bottom of the Word window. It shows information about the document, such as the page number, word count, and language settings. It also provides access to view modes like Print Layout and Web Layout.

## 4. Paragraph

A paragraph is a block of text in Word, usually separated by pressing the Enter key. Paragraphs can be formatted in terms of alignment, indentation, line spacing, and more.

## 5. Font

A font is the style of the text. Common fonts include Arial, Times New Roman, and Calibri. You can change the font style, size, and color to modify how your text looks.

## 6. Tab

A tab in Word refers to one of the main categories in the Ribbon, such as Home, Insert, or Design. Each tab contains specific tools to perform different tasks, like formatting text or adding images.

## 7. Header and Footer

The header is the area at the top of a page in Word, and the footer is at the bottom. These areas are used to display content like page numbers, document titles, or author names.

## 8. Margin

Margins are the blank spaces around the edges of a document. You can adjust the margins in Word to change the layout and appearance of your document.

# Common Terms in Microsoft Excel

## 1. Workbook

A workbook in Excel is a file that contains one or more worksheets. Each worksheet is a separate page where you can enter data, perform calculations, and create charts.

## 2. Worksheet

A worksheet is a single page within a workbook. It is made up of rows and columns, and you can enter, edit, and analyze data in each worksheet.

## 3. Cell

A cell is a single box in a worksheet where you can enter data. Each cell is identified by its row number and column letter, such as A1, B2, or C3.

## 4. Formula

A formula is an equation used to perform calculations on data in Excel. For example, the formula =SUM(A1:A5) adds the values in cells A1 through A5. Formulas always begin with an equals sign (=).

## 5. Function

A function is a pre-built formula in Excel that simplifies calculations. Examples of functions include SUM, AVERAGE, and VLOOKUP. Functions are a quick way to perform common tasks.

## 6. Cell Reference

A cell reference is a way of referring to a specific cell in Excel by its row and column coordinates. There are two types of cell references:

- Relative Cell Reference: Changes when the formula is copied to another cell. For example, A1 is a relative reference.
- Absolute Cell Reference: Does not change when the formula is copied. For example, $A$1 is an absolute reference.

## 7. Row and Column

Rows are the horizontal lines in an Excel worksheet, labeled with numbers (1, 2, 3, etc.). Columns are the vertical lines, labeled with letters (A, B, C, etc.). The intersection of a row and column creates a cell.

## 8. Chart

A chart is a graphical representation of data in Excel. Charts allow you to visualize data trends and patterns. Common types of charts include Bar Charts, Line Charts, and Pie Charts.

## 9. PivotTable

A PivotTable is a powerful tool in Excel that allows you to summarize, analyze, and present large amounts of data in a dynamic way. It helps you quickly find trends and patterns in your data.

## 10. Filter

A filter is a tool used to display only certain data in an Excel worksheet based on specific criteria. For example, you can filter a list of names to show only those starting with the letter "A."

## 11. Conditional Formatting

Conditional formatting is a feature in Excel that allows you to change the appearance of cells based on certain conditions. For example, you can set a rule to highlight cells that contain values greater than 100.

## 12. Data Validation

Data validation ensures that the data entered into a cell meets specific criteria. For example, you can set up a rule that only allows numbers between 1 and 100 to be entered into a cell.

## General Microsoft Word and Excel Terms

1. Template

A template is a pre-designed document or workbook that you can use as a starting point for your own projects. Both Word and Excel offer a variety of templates for different tasks, such as resumes, budgets, and reports.

2. Save vs. Save As

- Save: Saves the changes made to the current document or workbook.
- Save As: Creates a new copy of the document or workbook, allowing you to save it under a different name or file format.

3. File Format

A file format determines how a document or spreadsheet is saved and can be opened. For example, DOCX is the standard file format for Word documents, and XLSX is the format for Excel workbooks.

4. Formula Bar

The formula bar is located at the top of the Excel window. It displays the contents of the selected cell, allowing you to edit or enter new formulas and data.

## 5. Data Entry

Data entry refers to the process of inputting information into cells in Excel or typing text into a document in Word. Accurate data entry is essential for successful data analysis and document creation.

# Appendix D: Practice Exercises

---

Welcome to the practice exercises section! These exercises are designed to help reinforce the skills you've learned throughout the book. Each exercise is structured to give you hands-on experience with both Microsoft Word and Microsoft Excel. By completing these exercises, you'll be able to apply the concepts you've learned and gain confidence in using these applications effectively.

## 1. Document Formatting Challenge in Word

Objective:

Create a well-formatted document in Microsoft Word that includes headings, paragraphs, bullet points, and a table. The document will be a simple report that demonstrates your knowledge of formatting tools.

Steps to Complete the Exercise:

1.  Start a Blank Document
    Open Microsoft Word and start a new blank document.

2. Create a Title

   Type the title of your document at the top. For example, "My First Report."

   o Highlight the title text, choose the Heading 1 style from the Styles section in the Ribbon, and adjust the font size to 24.

3. Insert a Heading for the First Section

   Type "Introduction" as a heading for the first section of your document.

   o Use Heading 2 style to format this heading, and make it bold.

4. Write Paragraphs

   Below the "Introduction" heading, write two or three sentences introducing the topic of your report.

   o Align the text to the left using the Left Align button on the Home tab.

   o Apply line spacing of 1.5 for readability.

5. Add a Bullet List

   In the next section of your document, type "Key Features" and format it as a heading using Heading 2. Below this heading, create a bullet-point list of three key features of your chosen topic.

   o Use the Bullets button in the Paragraph group on the Ribbon to create the list.

6. Insert a Table

   After the bullet points, create a table with two columns and three rows. In the first column, type "Feature," and in the second column, type "Description."

   - Populate the table with information about the key features you mentioned earlier.
   - Apply Table Style to make the table visually appealing.

7. Final Formatting Adjustments

   - Add a page number to the footer of the document.
   - Adjust the margins to 1-inch on all sides by selecting Layout > Margins > Normal.
   - Save your document with the name "Formatted Report."

## 2. Simple Budget Creation in Excel

Objective:

Create a simple budget spreadsheet in Microsoft Excel. This exercise will help you practice working with data, basic formulas, and formatting.

Steps to Complete the Exercise:

1. Start a New Workbook

   Open Microsoft Excel and create a new blank workbook.

2. Create Column Headers

   In the first row, create the following column headers:
   - A1: "Expense Category"
   - B1: "Planned Amount"
   - C1: "Actual Amount"
   - D1: "Difference"

3. Enter Sample Data

   In the first column (A), list a few typical expense categories:
   - A2: "Rent"
   - A3: "Groceries"
   - A4: "Utilities"
   - A5: "Transportation"
   - A6: "Entertainment"

   In the second column (B), enter the planned amounts for each category:

   - B2: 1200
   - B3: 300
   - B4: 150
   - B5: 100
   - B6: 50

In the third column (C), enter the actual amounts you spent:

- C2: 1200
- C3: 280
- C4: 140
- C5: 110
- C6: 60

4. Calculate the Difference

   In the fourth column (D), you will calculate the difference between the Planned Amount and the Actual Amount for each category.

   - In D2, enter the formula =B2-C2 to find the difference between the planned and actual amounts for rent.
   - Copy this formula down from D2 to D6 to calculate the differences for all categories.

5. Apply Formatting

   - Bold the header row (A1 to D1).
   - Apply a Currency format to columns B, C, and D by selecting the columns and choosing Currency from the Number Format dropdown on the Ribbon.
   - Adjust the column width to make sure all the text is visible.

6. Final Touches

- o Use Conditional Formatting to highlight any differences in the "Difference" column that are negative. Select the range from D2 to D6, go to Home > Conditional Formatting > Highlight Cells Rules > Less Than, and enter 0 to format the cells with negative differences in red.

7. Save the Workbook

Save your workbook as "Budget.xlsx" for future reference.

# Index